Caring for Those Who Can't

Caring for Those Who Can't

Carol Dettoni

VICTOR BOOKS
A DIVISION OF SCRIPTURE PRESS PUBLICATIONS INC.
USA CANADA ENGLAND

Copyediting: Jerry Yamamoto, Barbara Williams
Cover Design: Scott Rattray
Cover Photo: Shoji Yoshida

Library of Congress Cataloging-in-Publication Data

Dettoni, Carol.
    Caring for those who can't / by Carol Dettoni.
       p.   cm.
    Includes bibliographical references.
    ISBN 1-56476-063-4
    1. Church work with the sick. 2. Caregivers—Religious life. 3. Family—Religious life. 4. Helping behaviour—Religious aspects—Christianity. 5. Love— Religious aspects—Christianity.
    I. Title.
    BV4460.D488   1993
    362.1'0425—dc20
                                       93-910
                                         CIP

---

1 2 3 4 5 6 7 8 9 10 Printing/Year 97 96 95 94 93

Acknowledgments

The following people have graciously shared from their personal and professional experiences, and have added to this book with great thoughtfulness. I am deeply grateful and hope that their experiences will benefit others who are caring: Elizabeth Brown, R.N., M.S.N. in geriatric nursing, Maitland, Florida; Dr. Marilyn Ditty, Director, South Coast Senior Services and Adult Day Care Center, San Clemente, California; Marsha Fowler, R.N., M.Div., Ph.D., Director of the Parish Nursing Program, Azusa Pacific University, Azusa, California; Kris Hollingbery, R.N., M.S.N., and Nursing Instructor, Yakima, Washington; Alana Peters, M.S.N., geriatric specialist, instructor, founder, and director, Care Options, Elder Care Management, and Caregiving Solutions, Irvine, California; Dr. Ronald Shackleford, Associate Minister, San Clemente Presbyterian Church, and owner of Oceanair Manor Board and Care Facility, San Clemente, California; Doris Stevens, minister's wife, Rancho Capistrano Church, San Juan Capistrano, California; Marjorie Stiles, R.N., San Clemente, California; Robert Vander Zaag, minister, financial consultant, and staff therapist for Christian Counseling Center, Laguna Niguel, California; Paul Van Oss, President of Board of Directors, Home of Hope Hospice, Grand Rapids, Michigan; caregivers who remain anonymous; family members; and others along the way who have shared from their experiences.

Dedication

To my father, Dr. Livius Poindexter McClenny:

Who cared for me throughout life
Who taught me about trusting and serving God with my whole being
Who modeled Christlike love throughout life, up to his last breath
Who witnessed about the love of Christ in a winsome way with boldness and courage
Who never complained, even when in the depths of pain and discomfort
Whose sense of humor and love for people was contagious
Who longed for heaven, yet loved life
Who spoke the truth and was a person of integrity, even when it cost him
Who sacrificed in order to be generous to family, friends, missionaries, and those in need
Who always said, "Remember, God is on the throne!"

To his other caregivers, my husband John and children Beth Ann and David; his daughters and sons-in-law Ann and Joe Sawyer, Patricia and Ben Hale, and Betty Jane and Steve Hull; and the other grandchildren: Jane Allison; Jonathan, Patricia, and Carolyn Sawyer; Brooks and John Hale, and Ruth and Nathan Hull.

To his special friends, givers of care and love: Dan and Lydia Bode, B.J. and Carole Cook, Ed and Alice Rink, Jack and Edie Shaffer, and the many friends and relatives whose cards, letters, and telephone calls kept him alive and full of hope.

To the doctors whom he loved who participated in his care: Bill Faust, M.D. and fishing partner and his wife Janie; Stuart Nagasawa, M.D., Michael Locke, M.D., and Bruce Tammelin, M.D., all of whom showed Christ's love with their outstanding medical expertise and their unusual concern and compassion.

Contents

Introduction

It's something you can't predict. One day your aging parent or other loved one is well, active, and vibrant. The next day he or she is hospitalized for exploratory surgery and biopsy, has been in a serious accident, has suffered a heart attack, or has been diagnosed with Alzheimer's or senile dementia, stroke, or another type of life-threatening crisis. Now that person is totally dependent on you for decision-making, health care, and the very practical matters of life.

It happens suddenly. Decisions must be made quickly, and other family members must be included in the planning and process of dealing with the crisis. The complexity of the situation is overwhelming. You are called upon to use inner resources and abilities you didn't know you had.

Somehow you muddle through from one day to the next. Not only are you learning new medical terminology and facing unfamiliar medical procedures, but you're also dealing with your own emotions and grief from the shock. At this point in your life you may have a career, be paying your children's college bills, or may have just begun to find discretionary time to pursue your lifelong dreams and interests. Or in the case of a stricken child, you may just be beginning a lifetime of dreams and hopes that is shattered in an instant. Everything comes to a shrieking halt, and life may never be the same. A woman, usually the primary caregiver, has nine months to prepare for childbirth, but virtually no preparation for such situations as these. In addition, a lifetime of experiences and emotions is wrapped up in the parent, child, or other loved one who is now dependent on you. In the case of an older person, you instantly take on the roles of the parent, a reversal that must be dealt with in a short amount of time. What do you do? Where do you find help? How can you learn all you need to know in a few hours or days in order to make wise decisions for your parent or relative, as well as for yourself and your immediate and extended family?

For almost three years, my life focused on some sort of caregiving or support-giving, and I had to struggle with these issues. First, for a year-and-a-half following my husband John's heart attack, my life focused on his recovery. Second, through a set of unusual circumstances I was court appointed as conservator for a very independent, at times unmanageable, ninety-four-year-old woman. Third, when my father was diagnosed with inoperable, terminal cancer, he moved in with our family. Overseeing his care became my privilege. All three members of my immediate family helped; each of us assisted in different parts of his care. And the other three of his daughters and family members took turns "spelling" me. My father underwent surgery, harsh chemotherapy, and radiation therapy, and many medical procedures before he died.

Through the many stages of accepting the cancer, looking for hope, discovering much about life, death, and God's continual presence with us, we have struggled and grown as a family. Our situation was unique in that our two single, young adult children lived at home while attending graduate school. Three generations faced daily changes, dependent on one another for strength, support, encouragement, humor, and assistance.

My experience was not unusual. In fact, it is becoming more and more common. It is estimated that parents spend approximately seventeen years caring for their children and eighteen years caring for their own parents.[1] The difference is that with children you know that, under normal circumstances, they will grow up.

Caregivers are mostly women; and with the grandparent boom, more caregivers are in their sixties.[2] Women assume the role of caregiver because it is expected of them; they have been brought up in a society where this is the norm. But society is changing. Millions of baby boomers will live long enough to be part of a great-grandparent boom, with an unprecedented number of eighty-five-year olds. When this happens in the early twenty-first century, a census report predicts that "five percent will be over this age. And the generation of very old baby boom survivors will be primarily women."[3] Although most caregivers are older women, there are millions of young adult women and male spouses caring for an aging loved one. In addition, "there are many seniors taking care of seniors."[4]

Already the numbers of caregivers are growing. A lot of people find themselves sandwiched between caring for their own children and caring for a parent or elderly relative at the same time. Over 4 million people were caregivers in 1991. Many of these are isolated and struggling, not realizing the resources that are available to them. And many experience burnout and poor health as a result. When asked the question, "Do you ever get angry enough that you might hurt the patient?" one-fifth of those caregivers answered, "Yes," because of stress and depression.[5]

Caregiving is also affecting the workplace. Caring for someone who can't care for himself or herself is an awesome and serious situation, so much so that even corporations are becoming more sensitive to the needs of their workers. The statistics show that "ten percent of all workers also serve as the primary caretakers for aging parents. Business executives are finding that workers without proper day-care arrangements are workers whose minds are not on their jobs. To help regain their attention, 137 major companies and organizations"[6] have announced a program to fund dependent care for employees' children and elderly relatives. And the number is growing.

"Elder care is a major social issue facing our nation today and is 'the sleeping giant' of the American workplace," according to gerontologist Alana Peters.[7] Since the number of caregivers in the workplace is growing so rapidly, employers are experiencing some extra costs "through higher incidents of: absenteeism and lateness; extended lunch hours; excessive telephone use during work hours; increased stress, anxiety, and depression; complaints about job dissatisfaction; increased turnover; on-the-job accidents; and health problems. Caring for the elderly is a commitment that doesn't stop on weekends and holidays, and it is a twenty-four-hours-a-day obligation."[8] The costs of elder care for an average-sized company can add up considerably.

The American Business Collaboration for Quality Dependent Care plans to fund 300 programs in forty-four communities in the United States, ranging from in-home arrangements for the elderly to day-care facilities. These kinds of programs acknowledge the severity of the situation, and will undoubtedly contribute greatly to the ever-growing problem of caring for those who are dependent on others.

Some of the elderly, particularly those with Alzheimer's and dementia, are neglected by their families, and stories of abuse are being told. "Social workers understand that caring for an aging, infirm relative day in and day out drains families, not just financially but physically and emotionally as well. The wonder is that so many people willingly shoulder the burden with fortitude and grace."[9]

The problems can be overwhelming. Our society as a whole faces some difficult decisions. In the midst of all this, how can the Christian family handle the challenge of caregiving? How does the Christian family follow the biblical principles of caring for others for whom they are responsible and draw upon the resources that society has to offer, while at the same time focusing on both its own and the patient's spiritual needs?

Being a caregiver seems to qualify that person for membership in a "special group." When former caregivers hear that I'm writing a book on the subject, they pull me aside and give a wistful, "I was a caregiver too" statement. There is an immediate bonding, an unspoken understanding, a deep sigh, and the body language of pain and sorrow. Emotions and remembrances are deep and tears well up instantly. Caregivers have had joy and sorrow. Yet most would not trade the experience and the personal growth for the world.

The following pages reflect mainly my experiences and

some responses from interviews with other caregivers. The book focuses primarily on caregiving for a spouse, an older parent, or relative. But much of the content can be adapted for shorter-term care and care for a younger person. The principles for caring for another person's life are the same—the demands and stresses are equally as overwhelming.

Other caregivers face similar issues, in similar situations, and have found as I did the unlimited resources that we have in our relationship with God as His children. At times it's hard to even express the very deepest feelings: the soul is bone dry; and the stresses and cares of caregiving demand every ounce of life. I pray that you may experience those unlimited resources upon which you can draw when the whole world seems to be falling apart.

Caring for my father—while one of the most difficult times—was one of the greatest joys of my lifetime, even including his very last breath as he was lifted to His eternal home.

PART ONE
A Family Matter

CHAPTER ONE
It Can't Be Happening!

My caregiving experiences first began when I was awakened by my husband, John, early on September 6, 1988: "Call 911! I think I'm having a heart attack!" John recovered from his full arrest and myocardial infarction, thanks to CPR administered by Eric Branstrom, a visitor in our home, and to efficient paramedics who gave two defibrillations and started the heart beating properly again. But for almost a year I learned what it's like to have another adult almost totally dependent on me—physically, emotionally, psychologically, and sometimes spiritually.

For the first time in my life, I experienced what it means to make decisions for another person, and how weighty and sometimes overwhelming that can be. I also discovered how ill-prepared I was to handle emergencies. Of course I had experienced caring for my own children, but that is another kind of caring—mothering, parenting, nurturing, leading, and guiding. You're preparing one for life, not possible debilitation of the body or even death, which involves a whole different set of emotional attitudes.

One year later, my second caregiving experience began. John and I went for a short trip to Tampa, Florida, he on business and I to visit my very young eighty-three-year-old father. Changing planes on an early morning flight in Chicago turned into an overnight delay. We were airport-bound in the heaviest snowfall in the shortest amount of time that Chicago had experienced this century. On the telephone my father sounded unusually disappointed that we were delayed. His voice was plaintive, almost clinging, very unlike his usually strong manner. I think he sensed something was seriously wrong with him.

When we finally arrived in Tampa, our escapade in the Chicago storm was overshadowed with my father's news: "I've got to go in for a biopsy. Do you mind going with me?"

Daddy strode into the hospital, taking the last truly strong, quick, and confident steps of his life. He looked handsome, twenty years younger than his actual age, and he cheerfully chatted and joked with nurses and staff. As always, people gravitated toward him. A simple biopsy turned into major exploratory surgery, and the shocking news was that the pain and shortness of breath he had suffered for many years was inoperable mesothelioma, cancer of the pleura caused by asbestos exposure.

Alone to Make Decisions

My husband had already returned home, and I was without family in the city. But my lifelong friend, Lillian Williams, was with me when the doctor gave the prognosis. She was strong and able to ask the questions that I could not think of in my shock. My father, "Dr. Mac," was a dearly loved minister and cared for by many. And as the word spread, many of his friends came to see him and pray with him. Somehow, I managed to make the telephone calls to my three sisters spread across the country. I remember the initial shock, the coldness of standing at a pay telephone in a waiting room filled with people, sharing such life-changing news while feeling so alone, scared, and helpless—and hopeless. I walked back and forth between my father's hospital room and the waiting room, where I made the many telephone calls, each time struggling to keep and regain my composure and "be strong for my father." It seemed at times surrealistic, a play being acted out on a cold and sterile stage. It was not—could not—be real. Yet it was.

Daddy awoke from surgery, still very drugged and groggy, but his eyes were alert and searching. I tried to avoid the "what did the doctor say" questions, leaving them for the surgeon to answer. Besides, I didn't fully understand all of the terminology. It's strange how you want to protect your loved one from the truth. (I learned from my mistake with John. Just minutes after he came out of a coma, I said, "You've had a heart attack, but you're fine." My doing that bothered him. It was too much to handle, too soon.) Thus, I needed wisdom—and a few hours to process what was happening.

In shock, I waited, trying to be positive on the outside while screaming on the inside. When the doctors came to him with their news, they tried to be both compassionate and honest. But the surgeon avoided the direct answer, "It is terminal." I nabbed him in the hall. After all, he was the one who had actually seen the cancerous tumor inside his chest. I wanted him to be the one to tell him. "Does he have long to live?" I asked directly. He still avoided a direct reply (doctors do have to protect themselves in this day of lawsuits), but he indicated it might be only a matter of weeks, if that long. The cancer was quite extensive. It had enveloped the right lung, squeezing it so that it was virtually ineffective.

Chemotherapy

Not too many minutes later, a strong and extraconfident oncologist arrived in a flurry. He described mesothelioma (his specialty) and glibly related how there was *no* hope of cure or remission. But he had used chemotherapy many times to try to give a better quality of life to his patients. In some cases it might make life more palliative. Palliative became the operative word from that time on. The statis-

tics he quoted, however, were not in favor of the procedure. My sisters questioned the value of chemotherapy
based on the statistics, but supported whatever our father
decided. Other family members who are in the medical
profession also questioned undergoing chemotherapy, trying to be objective from a distance. I passed on this information to my father. But a doctor whose demeanor alone
said to a patient, "Trust me!" as well as my father's desire
to be cooperative and hopeful, led my father down a route
that took him to his very lowest. He seemed like a lamb.
He wanted to try chemotherapy, and he trusted doctors
with their experience and knowledge.

I remember so well. There was a tube in Daddy's back,
draining the fourteen-inch incision. He had oxygen for
breathing, an IV in his arm for fluids and pain medication,
and an EKG monitoring his heart. He was still groggy from
the anesthesia and pain medication. And he had to make
the decision for a "go, no go" regarding the future of his
life.

The oncologist was authoritative and experienced. Although he said, "Think about it, and I'll come back tomorrow for your answer," tomorrow came and the doctor
didn't. The next thing we knew, my father was having a
port-a-catheter implanted in his shoulder for IVs, drawing
blood for testing, and administering chemotherapy. (This
turned out to be a God-send for future pricks and sticks,
for the patient's comfort and convenience.) If I had had
even a bit more time to interact and reflect with my father,
given the advice that we had received from many people,
Daddy may have made a different decision. He had always
said, "I'll never go through chemotherapy, unless it will
truly make a difference." But when the moment came, he
either didn't get a clear picture of his condition or he
wanted to live so much that he decided to try the therapy.

I realized I had to take control of the situation and of his
life, as much as he needed and allowed me to do. Facing
this reality was one of my hardest moments as a caregiver.
I had to begin to parent my parent. I had to take charge. I

gathered my strength, cried out to God for help, and began asking the doctors questions. I took copious notes so that I could communicate details to my sisters and extended family members. My primary concern became my father and his well-being. I had to be strong for him, and I learned quickly to go ahead and let some medical professionals feel threatened by my note taking and desire to know as many answers as possible. I had no time to play diplomatic games while my father took the brunt of the decisions. When I told my father that one doctor wrote in his paperwork, "Daughter takes notes all the time," he actually seemed proud of me and found it amusing!

At first we did not know and understand our options. We later learned what palliative care really means from my father's California oncologist, Dr. Stuart Nagasawa. Since that time we have found that more and more doctors are realizing that palliative care is preferable to using chemotherapy for those with no chance of recovery, as was my father's case.

Palliative Care

The standard of care for cancer in the United States is to "give some form of chemotherapy even though everyone knows all those patients are usually dead within a few months," according to oncologist Declan Walsh, Director of the Cleveland Clinic's palliative care program. "I am unaware of any study that demonstrates that chemotherapy in that context significantly improves the quality of life or indeed the duration of life to anything that would appear worthwhile."[1] The tragedy of this ethic is that it causes many doctors to offer—and patients to accept—aggressive treatment when their time could be better spent in palliative care. Unfortunately for my father, he did undergo harsh chemotherapy. In addition, he received radiation treatment to open his esophagus, which allowed him to enjoy a few additional months of life in a comparatively comfortable physical condition. In hindsight, I wish I had been stronger in opposition to using chemotherapy because it takes a person so low physically. In situations such as my father's, with statistics indicating no hope, it turned out to be impossible for him to truly regain strength. For the body to overcome the effects of brutal chemicals and recover from surgery was indeed an uphill battle for even a palliative existence. And particularly so at age eighty-three.

The realization of what was happening hit hard when I was alone in my father's home the first night after the biopsy. Daddy had always been so strong; he always took care of me. I, as eldest, however, cleaned his wounds when he first arrived home after my mother had been killed in a car accident while he was driving. There were many other firsts that the eldest experiences in any family. Now, he was almost totally dependent on me. Not only did I cry tears of grief at the news, but I also felt hopelessly inadequate. I felt I had to take charge, and I didn't want to do that.

There were many sleepless, tearful nights ahead, including the terrible night I had chest pains and trouble breathing, no doubt a physical and emotional response to the stress and grief. I had to tell myself to get a grip and trust God's healing power and comfort in His best plan for my father and for me. The tears often became dry and almost retching. Looking back on those days, I realize that the tears and grief were good to experience at that time. I was able to move on to the next part of life, that of being strong and mostly in control of these extreme emotions around my father. However, I do believe that crying with him at times allowed him to express his feelings too. Precious moments for each of his caregivers were experienced when we talked and cried about life and death. Being in control of my emotions also enabled me to help others share and process their grief. We took turns crying and grieving, but for the most part allowed the caregiving environment to be a joyful, peaceful place of love and concern.

Special Relationships

All four of his daughters had special relationships and unique bonds with Daddy. Each one wanted him to move and live with her. And each handled grief in a very individual way. We all supported one another for decision-making and by being there when needed. I must say that my three sisters would have taken the responsibility for Daddy. I, as eldest, was able to have him move in with us because of our housing setup and the fact that our children were adults. It was a family decision that the four of us made, and the other three sisters supported me in an unbelievably positive and loving way. My sisters were able to have a part in their father's caregiving as much as their family and work responsibilities allowed.

When my father came to live with us, he was in such pain that he could not sit in a chair for more than a few minutes. So we purchased three recliners. One chair went in the living room where he could look out the window. Another was in the den so he could watch television and videos with the family. And one was in his bedroom so he could sleep and watch television comfortably there.

We talked, prayed, took short rides together, and laughed. I saw a sense of humor that I had never known before. And we all enjoyed life. Daddy made a great admission when he said that he wished he had moved closer to one of his daughters sooner. We rearranged our lives to fit his needs. All four of us, John and I and our two young adult children, changed our living habits—television programs, social lives, eating habits, and personal desires—to focus on his needs and his time with us. We each had a role to play in his life, and we enjoyed it to the fullest. There was, however, always that nagging knowledge that his time with us was short. The pain and suffering were always obvious and put an edge on most situations.

How did the family react? Each of my three sisters has written their feelings toward the cancer, toward me, and toward their relationship with Daddy. Ann writes:

When Carol called me and told me that Daddy had cancer, I did not deny that it was so, but knew that it would be all right and that he would get over it. Daddy, to me, was almost immortal. There was no way that this would harm him, because I felt that I needed him. Truly very illogical reasoning!

After going to Florida to be with him while he went through a round of chemotherapy, watching him get sick, listening to him talk about what I should do in the future with family members, I got really angry. It wasn't fair—he shouldn't be sick, therefore he wasn't sick.

After I returned home I was still determined that he would get well. We had to get him to the most progressive hospital in the country, with the best doctors in the world. I knew for a fact that no one would be able to take care of him like I would, that no one loved him as much as I did, and that he definitely loved me best of all. It was several weeks until I had peace inside of me that he was where he should be, that the decision to continue with chemotherapy was the right one, that he should be with Carol, and that he really may not get well.

When I would go to help take care of Daddy, I found that Carol was the authority figure. Daddy would say to me, "Carol won't let me have this; may I?" It got to be a game for both of us, to see what we could get away with. But when I tried to get him to do something that he didn't want to do, like take some Ensure (food supplement) or medicine or go for a walk, he would say, "Carol doesn't want me to do that," or "Carol said I should try going without that stuff." It was frustrating!

For me, the hardest part of caregiving was to see Daddy physically deteriorate, to have to take care of him in the more personal aspects—bathing and helping him with the daily bodily functions. When the older person's mind is sharp, it makes it so very hard to keep them from being totally humiliated.

In caring for both Daddy and for our daughter, Jane, following her accident, I have had feelings of being "put upon," of being used, of not being capable of performing the necessary tasks required to care for the sick one. My feelings are very selfish — I want Daddy back, I need him to help me. I find I want this for me.

The bottom line of caregiving for me is that the more you love someone, the easier it is to do the difficult. If the situation became unbearable, I could leave briefly and come back to start over with no problem.

I still have regrets at decisions I helped Daddy make, such as the trip to Alaska that he had planned. I still think that I should have been with him more, that I shirked in some way a responsibility to help care for him. Having him alive gave me someone to tell me "what to do," let me continue to be "the child" and lean on him. Since his death, I have been forced to depend on God more.

No Panic or Denial

Another sister, Patricia, responded to our father's biopsy in a matter-of-fact way, without panic or denial. She recognized the situation and the immediate knowledge that the cancer was terminal. For her, when our father left his own home to move in with us, "there was a finality to that. At that point, I did my grieving and acceptance of his situation."

The hard thing for Patricia, as well as for some of the rest of the family, was feeling as though he knew initially what the outcome was, that the illness was terminal, but realizing that

he was not realistic in talking about and accepting it, and that was unlike him. That was hard on me, because I was used to being open with him and, all of a sudden, I couldn't be. I felt like he may have said and done things because he was trying to get well — denial in a sense. We were in two different places: I was so used to being able to share and pray with him, and now we couldn't with the same openness. At this point, I grieved.

Betty Jane, the youngest sister, wrote:

When I learned that Daddy had cancer, I was angry and did not believe it. My lingering thought was "he's gone through so much already with my mother's death in a car accident and his illness with a brain tumor. Why this? He's so young at heart and always doing things."

When it was my turn to take care of Daddy, I was frightened that he would die because of something I might do wrong, or something I might fail to do to care for him. My emotions were hard to handle — I couldn't stand to see him in pain and unable to walk much or sleep well. When he visited me in our Washington state home for the last time, I felt so helpless; he was in such pain. I wanted him to return to Carol's so he could be near his doctors.

What did we learn from all of this? Most importantly, as his immediate and extended family, we confirmed and re-discovered the importance of the family unit. How thankful and blessed we are to have family and friends that care! We also realized how God the Father cares for His family. Like the Good Shepherd, He tends His flock, and we can find comfort in that even if there is not a supportive, help-ful family network during the difficult times.

We learned how very important it is to sit at the patient's bedside, to listen, and to love. These can be gentle, contem-plative, and caring times of one's life. It's a special gift for a caregiver to be allowed this most intimate experience.

Other Caregiver Stories

Other caregivers share similar stories—ones that show the loving support from family and lessons of love in caregiving. Marjorie Stiles traveled from Southern California to Arizona every two weeks for two-and-a-half years to give her father a five-day respite from caring for her mother, who suffered from senile dementia. She says:

> It was so hard—Dad had shielded us from knowing how bad the situation was, because mother would oftentimes be fine. She would forget that she had acted in an irrational manner. When we discovered this, it was really hard to deal with. By this time Dad was ready for a total collapse. He had her total care, and she'd be up at night. So it was twenty-four hour care. I would leave in tears because my mother, who had always been reaching out to those in need, was not herself. It was so hard to see her this way.
>
> My mother had cared for her mother for thirty-five years. She had said, "I never want to go to a nursing home." I always replied, "No, Mother, of course not." It was only through a lot of prayer that we were able to put her in a nursing home when the doctor told us: "Either you must put her in a nursing home or you will lose your dad too." After Mother adjusted, she was happy where she was. But I felt the guilt, and other family members added to that guilt. They felt that because I didn't care for her at home, I didn't *care*. This has been painfully hard.

Coming to the point of giving up the care is sometimes equally as difficult as the long days of caregiving at home. Doris Stephens says,

> Putting my mother in a nursing home was so hard on me. We brought her to live in a nursing home close to us. I went every other day and would help with her

care when I saw a need. There were over ten patients for each aide. There was never enough help. It took two to three people to move her. So it was impossible for me to care for her at home.

When a Young Person Needs Care

Caring for a child or young adult who is suffering from a disease or an accident is a very difficult situation for families. Unlike caring for the elderly person who is expected to die soon, the parent has the added emotions of "Why does this happen to my child, who has life ahead for him or her?"

My sister Ann also experienced caregiving when her eldest daughter, Jane was hit by an out-of-control car and nearly died from her injuries.

I experienced similar but sometimes different feelings and emotions than those experienced caring for my father. Jane was only fifteen when it happened. Her leg was so badly shattered that she almost lost it and her life. After many, many surgeries, muscle flap transplants and skin grafts, she is finally able to walk and live a normal life. But her lifestyle is greatly altered. She can never play sports again, wear most kinds of shoes, and will have problems for her lifetime. Taking care of her for the year — she was virtually homebound — was often an extreme chore. I feel that I neglected the other three children and my husband. I truly didn't think that anyone else could take care of her as well as I could. Many times I felt like a robot going through the motions of life.

There were times when Jane was angry — but only at me. When company would come into the room, she was sweet as she could be to them. As soon as they would leave, she would explode. Her doctor had told me at the very beginning that this would happen, that she would have to work through her frustrations, and that it would be taken out on me, her mother. There is still great anger, even today. I still find it hard to balance all of the feelings, both mine and those close around me.

The physical part of caring for Jane was hard, but it was the emotional part that became the most difficult to cope with. There was anger, not at the driver of the car or at God—just anger. There was fear—of what, I don't know. It still comes, even at the most unexpected times and in unusual situations. I do believe the mental and emotional caregiving, particularly in this instance, is harder than the physical.

A Young Patient's Experience

Jane, now a young adult and mother, recalls her feelings:

The first thing I would tell parents of a hospitalized child, no matter what the age of the child, is that somehow our mind does not remember trauma. I believe God, with compassion and grace, designed us to eliminate it from our memory. I remember pain and fear, but it was from the series of seemingly endless blood tests, x-rays, and checkups. My son was recently hospitalized and operated on at the age of five weeks. The peace that I clung to was knowing from experience that he would not remember the pain and trauma of an IV and surgery.

As a patient at age fifteen, my fondest memories were of my friend, Chris, sitting with me in my hospital room. Sitting, that's all. So many people felt they had to talk or entertain me, when all it did was wear me out! As soon as I heard visitors walking toward my room I would put my headphones on without turning on the radio and close my eyes so they would talk to my mother instead. This is one of the many times my mom saved me.

Every patient needs someone to confide in. For me

that person was my mother. When I needed privacy, she met visitors at the door to my room, talked with them, and then sent them on their way. Don't get me wrong—visitors are wonderful. Their timing, however, isn't always great.

My mother was also the person who bore the brunt of my anger and fear. My doctor told her that she would be yelled at, shunned one minute and wanted the next, and she was. Had I known what I was doing I never would have treated her that way. Had I known. Remember, not only is an illness physical but also it is mental. Add to the pain killers, antibiotics, a variety of other medications, and in most cases physical therapy—fear. Fear of what's happening to your body, your lifestyle, your future.

Thus, as a parent caring for your very sick child, let him or her lash out, don't say anything in reply, and then leave the room to cry. By the time you are ready to return, your child will be wondering why it took you so long to "get a cup of coffee." (That was my mother's excuse for leaving the room.) There were rare moments when I realized what I had done and apologized. I think that one of the rewards for all of the hardship I put her through was that she was the first one to hear about an accomplishment I made in my progress, because I wanted her to be the first to know.

Mother was my best friend through my high school years—the time when she cared for me. But then I went to college. The closeness was wonderful, but a child needs friends his or her own age. So, after my recovery, when I started making friends, my mother was left out. As a parent caring for a very sick or injured child, you invest so much time, energy, and emotion into your child that it becomes a way of life. When that effort is no longer needed, a void takes its place. All of a sudden I wasn't confined to a bed or wheelchair. I wanted to do everything I had not been able to do for an entire year. With whom? My old friends were all in athletics, and that was out for me. One girl I knew was in a crisis over what to wear to Homecoming. I couldn't relate. I guess the best thing my parents did for me then was make opportunities for me to get involved. They didn't let me sit around and feel sorry for myself. If one event didn't work, we tried another.

Before the accident, I had centered my life around athletics in school; now I could never even run again. Once that reality hit, my father jumped at the chance to draw out a talent that he had seen in me — art. My hospital room was filled with pencils and drawing paper. I think the most important part of this was Dad's timing. Had he tried before I had acknowledged and dealt with the fact that I could no longer play any sport, I wouldn't have listened. Not only did I listen, but I also graduated from college with a degree in fine arts and continue to use it both in my career and for fun.

Let brothers and sisters visit the patient. Not only did it help me, but also it helped them. One of my sisters was afraid of anyone in the family leaving and never returning. Visiting me helped reassure her that I was still alive. Children (my brothers and sisters were thirteen, ten, and seven) are able to handle more than adults sometimes. I was in traction, had an IV, and sometimes drainage tubes from surgery. They didn't seem to notice them as much as adults. In their innocence, since they saw it as helping me, they left it at that.

We joked a lot. I had "smile therapy" daily. We joked about what I was going through — my scars, the contraptions the doctors put me in. To this day, I would rather someone say, "Your ankle is ugly; but at least you have one," than to stare and not say a word. Parents, be sensitive to those who stare and let your child know that you saw it too and how much it hurts.

Here are some ideas for parents of an injured or sick child: (1) If, for your peace of mind, you need to sit with your child, sit. (2) Listen. (3) Run interference for him or her. (4) Let your child know what is happening; it is his or her body, and information is needed for the child's peace of mind. (5) Laugh and joke. The seriousness of the illness is enough to handle. (6) Encourage, but be realistic about the situation. God will never give a person more than he or she can handle. (7) Let your child help others during the illness. I gave stuffed animals and balloons to younger children who were patients. (8) Point out hidden talents. (9) Brighten the atmosphere; keep the windows open. (10) Bring t-shirts for your child to sleep in instead of those ugly, humiliating hospital gowns. (11) Don't take books for your child to read. The medication makes it impossible to real.

My grandfather told me, "There are no accidents with God, only incidents." There is a plan for everything. That didn't make it any easier, but it reminded me that God loves me and challenges me daily to find out what that plan might be.

Bob Vander Zaag and his wife, Glenda, were pastoring a church in the East when their young daughter, Cheryl, contracted polio. Cheryl, now a very active and beautiful young adult, has learned to live a very productive life with her disability and is, in fact, in graduate school. However, it was quite traumatic for the family to handle in the early years, and there were many struggles for each of them. For instance, for years the older daughter carried a sense of guilt that she could walk normally and Cheryl could not. Only as an adult could she begin to express this feeling. Bob says,

Our immediate family was crucial to our survival. We leaned heavily on one another. Our families were only marginally helpful since the closest was over four hundred miles away and really had no idea what we were going through. Because of our isolation from the rest of our families, our immediate family has been much closer than most.

The one constant in all the examples of caregiving is that it is a difficult job. Christians, however, have the advantage of knowing that they have spiritual resources — indeed, that God's Spirit, the ultimate Caregiver, will sustain and provide as they learn and grow through the difficulties of life.

CHAPTER TWO
A Week in the Life of a Caregiver

You've coped with the initial shock. Your tears have dried, although the grief and pain reside in a deep well ready to spurt out at unexpected moments. For the most part, however, since life is moving ahead at a frenetic pace, you continue to cope. This time it is with uncertainty, harboring feelings ranging from total inadequacy to anger to despair to peace to helplessness to stoic resolution—and sometimes all in one day!

Flexibility, shifting gears, going with the flow—a caregiver must employ all of these characteristics. Why? Because every day, every week, is different for the caregiver and the care receiver. Nothing is ever predictable. This includes not only the ups and downs of the recipient, but also the physical, emotional, and spiritual roller coaster on which a caregiver rides. For many recipients, particularly the terminally ill or those undergoing an ongoing treatment such as chemotherapy, radiation therapy, and dialysis, life consists of daily medications, food to be eaten and drunk, a little television, a trip or two for medical treatment, a doctor's office visit, an unexpected physical change, and whatever other small diversions may arise. The caregiver must see that all of these activities are planned for and accomplished. The caregiver is the encourager, the giver of hope and joy, the social director, the cook, and the nurse. In addition, the caregiver has a need and desire to simply enjoy being with the recipient. At times, however, it just doesn't all fit together.

The recipient truly bears the biggest burdens. We must not overlook that fact. He or she experiences the decaying of the body and endures pain and suffering. In addition, the feeling that one is being a burden is difficult for many to handle. Facing the end of one's life or major changes in one's future brings tremendous uncertainties, no matter how spiritually minded and full of trust the patient may be. These factors should not be underestimated and lost in a book on caregiving. If the needs of the patient are not the focus and the number one driving force of the caregiver, then major areas of adjustment must be identified and made. The recipient is and should be of primary concern.

Walk with me now through a composite, typical week, taken from my calendar records. (I had, of course, no time to actually record my thoughts and feelings, just enough time to record doctor's appointments and daily medical information.) This week is excerpted from earlier caregiving stages of caregiving in the patient's decline, before my father was totally dependent and bedridden.

Monday

7:30 A.M. John, Beth Ann, and David prepare to leave for their eighty-mile commute. We try to have prayer as a family before they leave. Since I am attempting to maintain some of my roles in the family system, I fix bag lunches. David has taken the responsibility for praying with his grandfather each morning, and this activity has become a special time for the two of them.

Monday, Wednesday, and Friday: These days are for radiation treatments at the doctor's office, a fifteen-minute drive. The treatments themselves only last a few minutes. But just getting there takes my father's total energy for the day. He showers and dresses, then rests for a while before breakfast. He has already had coffee, juice, and medicine in the early morning hours. Sometimes he gets up and takes his medicine himself. When he can't manage, I take it to him in his bedroom. But he's determined to walk when he can and to eat, even though he has no appetite.

8:30 A.M. At breakfast there are more medications to be taken with food, roughage to be eaten for regularity (a major problem with patients undergoing chemotherapy or radiation therapy), and high protein food. After breakfast and a half-hour rest, he builds up enough energy to walk down the hall and prepare for the ride to the doctor's.

9:30 A.M. Traveling in the car is quite a task. We always take pillows for comfort, some to prop up his arm and one for behind his neck. We bring juice for him to drink in case of low blood pressure and dizziness, a couple of crackers, a sweater in the event it is too cool in the doctor's office, and medication for extreme pain or an emergency. I always plan for the unexpected event—suppose a flat tire or car trouble should leave us stranded by the freeway? It reminds me of the days when we took such things for short trips with our children.

My father proudly and with great dignity—a true gentleman to the end—opens my car door and struggles to walk into the doctor's office on his own. It is only a few steps from the car. (We have finally gotten a handicapped parking sticker—for many weeks he did not want to use one, because he "did not need it.")

Seeing the doctor, the technicians and the warm, friendly receptionist is always uplifting, even though the circumstances are grim. This connection with people is a lifeline to the outside world. They chat about life, their families, and their activities, and Daddy responds in kind with humor and warmth. Today he is due to get a CBC (complete blood count) and have his port-a-catheter heparinized. So we take a wheelchair ride up four floors and wait our turn for the laboratory work. Again, his friends, the doctor and nurses are glad to see him. (I am thankful that the medical personnel in these departments are, for the most part, so upbeat and congenial with their patients.) By now, the short radiation treatment has turned into a full morning's outing, and the ever-present pain is beginning to set in again. He takes some medication (usually morphine), and we take an elevator ride back to return the wheelchair.

The short walk to the car now seems like a mile-long hike. And the fifteen-minute ride home is a cross-country adventure. We listen to praise tapes, hymns, or soothing classical music, which keeps the ride from being too long and arduous. We play a game together, seeing how many times I can avoid hitting the bumps (the lane dividers) when I change lanes. We laugh and talk about things we see along the wayside, the scenery, or deep things in life. I treasure these trips, as difficult as they are, because I have a chance to visit with my father during these brief rides in a way that is not possible with the distractions of caregiving.

11:30 A.M. At home, it's back to the recliner and time to drink some Gatorade for low blood pressure or to have a special milk shake (I try to sneak in extra protein). He needs these drinks at least four times each day to keep up his strength and get the proper nutrition. He takes more medication with his shake and then rests in his living room chair for about an hour. During that hour I try to get some wash done, clean up his room and make his bed, and prepare lunch.

12:30 P.M. Daddy is not hungry, but he nibbles at his food, trying hard to eat enough. Trying to be creative and cook appealing food is the hardest of the practical caregiving details for me. (Because of our family's need for low-cholesterol/low fat diets, I've shifted my mind-set and no longer even think in terms of meats, fat, and the kinds of food my father likes and enjoys. We eat sprouts, vegetables, soybean substitutes, yogurt, tofu, Japanese rice, fish, turkey, and chicken. So I teetertotter from one culture to another, and it's tremendously challenging.) When my sister and other relatives come to visit him, I gladly encourage them to go into the kitchen to cook!

There's more medicine to be taken with lunch—an anti-inflammatory, stool softeners, iron pills, pain medication (at this point in his pilgrimage, he is still alternating between pain tablets and morphine). After lunch, the mail comes and a few cards arrive for him. He receives enough mail and telephone calls each week to help him feel missed, yet connected with his friends, neighbors, and family. Since he never has lived here, he has only a few friends in our area. The cards and letters from his friends around the country are his lifeline and his support.

1:30 P.M. Daddy doesn't feel like reading or watching television. And he doesn't feel like writing. So he snoozes and watches the hummingbirds' aerial dogfight outside the windows. We've hung two additional feeders for his enjoyment. He sits in his recliner and turns his chair to see life going on outside. He sometimes listens to a tape. But mostly he just sits, thinks, reads short Bible passages and prays, snoozing between times.

2:30 P.M. Another dosage of pain medication is needed, and I offer him some fruit paste (a prune concoction for constipation. See recipe in chap. 5). He needs to eat again with his medicine—it's an all-day process.

3:00 P.M. Our next-door neighbor, Alice Swanson, comes by to talk about genealogy and to visit with him. They have discovered a common interest, and she brings great joy. She only stays about one-half hour, a very appropriate length of time. Her quiet enthusiasm brightens up his day. I serve them a cup of tea and a cookie, and then take advantage of the time to run to the grocery store.

4:00 P.M. I hurry home. It's time for more pain medication and another shake (three in the daytime and one at night). My father naps until supper time. Sometimes he needs help getting in and out of his chair because the lever for the recliner is on the right side, the side of his body where the cancer resides. The pain he endures in just reaching for the lever is intense. I try to stay nearby to help him stand up. When his blood pressure is low, I walk with him to the bathroom. If I'm upstairs, he rings a bell to beckon me. (Early on, we buy three portable intercom units, and that helps us keep in touch throughout the house.) Today he walks to the bathroom. It's such an accomplishment to see him standing and walking on his own. His face beams with pride!

5:00 P.M. We take a four-block ride to see the ocean. We park at the top of the bluff, where we sit watching the surfers, the birds, the seals, and the interesting characters who frequent this spot. It's a touch with the outside world: families and children, people walking their dogs, teenagers, surfers, and picnickers. It's usually too cool and breezy to get out of the car, but once in a while we sit on a bench and enjoy the air. This fifteen-to-twenty-minute outing is crucial for both of us. I treat it as if we are going on a long trip. We take a special gel cushion to sit on, a pillow to prop his arm, the binoculars, medication, juice, and crackers. Always be prepared—that's my constant concern.

6:00 P.M. The two of us eat supper together. I fix simple fare—mashed potatoes, a vegetable, and meat. Since there's not a lot of time to cook, I mostly make things in the microwave. After supper, my father switches rooms and chairs for the evening.

6:30 P.M. We watch the news. It is a time of upheaval, and most of it is hard to watch. But Operation Desert Storm is being talked about and prepared for, and that provides a fascinating distraction. Since some people whom he knows may be involved, he spends time praying for them.

7:00–8:00 P.M. "Wheel of Fortune" and "Jeopardy" are on television. The fun of watching these two programs together, trying to answer the questions, and evaluating the winners becomes a nightly ritual.

8:00 P.M. A National Geographic nature special (a mellow and interesting program) is on TV. I fix another shake to drink with more medication. The pain is much worse at night, and television is not enough of an escape to distract him from his pain.

9:00 P.M. Daddy begins to prepare for bed. He dreads the nighttime and doesn't sleep much. He has a radio and tape player by his bedside, along with his medications and written instructions: "If the pain is really intense, take 3 cc of roxanol, but don't take it sooner than 1:00 A.M." I fix a tray of crackers, juice, and water for him each night. He also has a bell to ring in case he needs me. (He would not use the intercom until later on in his illness. I never could understand why.) In the kitchen I prepare his mug, coffee, and juice so that he can fix them for himself in the early morning, should he have the energy to do so.

10:00 P.M. John, Beth Ann, and David arrive home from their commute, just in time to hug, talk briefly, and say "good night." Daddy plans it so that he is still up when they arrive.

10:15 P.M. John helps Daddy get into bed and prays with him. These are special moments for each of them, and Daddy depends on this time, looking forward to it each night.

My caregiving is over for the day. I collapse into bed, but I never sleep soundly. On good nights, when he has the energy, Daddy gets up on his own several times. I hear him and listen for his door to shut. In the morning I will check the records and be sure he has managed his medications appropriately. Sometimes he can. Sometimes he doesn't have the energy and will ring for me. (Later on in his illness, he will simply begin to touch the intercom button, and I will shoot out of bed. I always have clothes ready to jump into in case of an unexpected trip to the emergency room, a habit I began after John's heart attack and continue to do to this day.)

Tuesday

More of the same, except that Daddy sleeps a bit more in the morning after breakfast. Since he was awake most of the night, these short catnaps throughout the day are crucial.

Today he is having a lot of intestinal/stomach pain. A call to the pulmonary specialist reveals that a short office visit is necessary. Again, even though the office is only five minutes away, we prepare for a trip. A wait in a doctor's office is never predictable. We discover that the anti-inflammatory medicine is probably causing irritation to his system and must be discontinued. He will try another medication for a week.

We make two stops on the way home, one to pick up dry cleaning and the other to drop off the prescription. We need to get home because he's in a lot of pain. While my father rests and sleeps, I run out to get the medicine. There are miscellaneous things to be done, and we try to take care of them as efficiently as we can.

Since my father's clothes are becoming too tight, I ask one sister to help find some more comfortable and practical ones. I just can't manage to do that on top of everything else.

There are business matters to care for. My father must pay his bills, and insurance forms and data need to be sorted through. He begins and tries to keep up. But he can't concentrate and finish. So I sit with him and help do the writing at his dictation.

He's too tired today for a ride to the ocean. He snoozes instead.

Wednesday

Radiation again. Since Daddy's having trouble swallowing, the radiation oncologist examines him today. We are to keep an eye on things. The doctor tells us that we need to change the diet a bit and drink and eat softer, more liquid foods. So I have to get out to the grocery store and buy new food. Today we go for a short ride—this time to a park, but we don't get out of the car.

Daddy's very discouraged. I give a sister a call and ask her to call him. We have prearranged this routine as a common procedure since my sisters are not around to see when such a telephone visit is needed. These calls always encourage him, and he always encourages them too.

Thursday

The weather is changing. Since my father feels cool, we need to get a space heater. We also pick up a flannel shirt for him to wear around the house. We invest in flannel sheets — a great purchase.

John is home today, but both kids work part time when they don't attend school. So John, Daddy, and I take a forty-five-minute round trip to the harbor. We pick up a sandwich and have a picnic on a bench. We watch the boats coming in and out, the people fishing from the jetty, and the sea gulls and pelicans diving and gorging on fish. It's a wonderful outing, but Daddy's intense pain and wooziness bring us back to reality.

Friday

His swallowing is bad, and we skip a day of radiation. Appetite has decreased dramatically, and energy is waning. It happened so quickly. Life for a cancer patient is fragile. The doctor says to come to the hospital — via the emergency room — for some IV fluids, an esophogram and an upper GI. This turns into a twelve-hour visit by the time Daddy is admitted to a room, and the doctor examines him and prescribes orders for medications. Then we wait through the tedious time, watching the IV fluid slowly give him strength again. (I bring pain medications from home to be given only with the hospital's knowledge. And I always take my paperwork wherever I go, along with some crocheting or handwork. And I just sit with Daddy.) The three-person treatment rooms are depressing, and I established early on that a person needs to accompany the patient, ask questions, and take charge overall. I eat hospital food in the room and take brief walks to see the infant nursery (a way to put life and death into perspective). Since we're at the hospital until after 10:00 P.M., the nightly routine is off a bit. And since the hospital bed is not as comfortable as a recliner, it's sheer joy to be back in the cozy comforts of home.

Saturday

Beth Ann is home and helps relieve some of the shake-making and medication-giving. I catch up on household necessities. Beth Ann always brings lightness to her grand-father with her *joie de vivre* attitude. David and John also spend extra time helping on the weekends and in the evenings. Each has different gifts and interests to share with Daddy. All three help cook, sit and visit, and watch television with him, as well as interact on subjects of mutual interest. They bring a fresh breath of air to the house while I try to keep my life in order. Each of us has a role to play, and we help one another out as we see the needs arise.

Sunday

We watch two church programs on television; they have become his church. (Daddy, with one exception, never made it to church after his biopsy and diagnosis. If he had a bad Saturday night, I always videotaped the service for him. That way he could watch it at his leisure. Depending on the events of the night before, I sometimes attended church or sometimes I spent Sunday mornings at home with him. For the most part, for about a year I was very irregular in church attendance because I was either too tired from being up all night, or my father was too ill to be left alone.)

The highlight of Sunday afternoons is the weekly trip that John and Daddy take to the harbor. (Sometimes I tag along.) Watching the boats come in and weigh their catch is the chief attraction. Today at a special spot they watch private yachts weigh their marlin catches. They try to guess the weight of each fish before it is registered on the deck.

Although each member of the family has a role to play,

we do help one another as well. The unpredictable daily schedule keeps us flexible and helps us learn to trust God in new ways. If the truth be known, there was no such thing as a typical week. Several times David helped me take Daddy to the emergency room in the middle of the night. Beth Ann backed me up in the hospital room when I needed to take a break and be at home, and she was on the spot when a need arose. She became the "assistant caregiver," with a very tender, soft touch. John, when time permitted, ran errands and made purchases I could not manage. The total family unit stepped in to cook, shop, give medications, chauffeur, and back one another up as their time, work, and study schedules allowed. They were remarkably understanding, and each day was flexed to include Daddy in our lives. (At one point, my father said he wished he had moved in with us sooner, because he felt so much a part of our family. This statement was really unexpected, because he had balked and protested during previous years when we begged him to move, either to live with us or near one of his other daughters.)

We put aside most of our personal social life and activity. We concentrated on being with Daddy and Grandfather, and there was really no time for anything else. For the most part, Beth Ann and David put their personal lives "on hold." (And, I might add, in retrospect, they have no regrets.)

Each day, each week for the caregiving family is a challenge. One day at a time, with God's grace and provision for strength and wisdom, is the caregiver's hope.

PART TWO
Taking Charge

CHAPTER THREE
What Do I Need to Know?

If I could tell you only one thing to remember, it would be this: Life is a special gift from God. The young anticipate it; but when an accident or illness alters their normal development, life and death take on new meanings. And for the dying Christian, under normal circumstances—no matter how much he or she wants to go to heaven to be with the Lord—there is still within his or her being a clinging to that God-given gift of life. This was quite startling for me to realize; I had never thought about it. I always expected that when one is diagnosed with a terminal illness, after dealing with the inevitability of one's mortality, the focus changes to, "I want to die and go to be with my Heavenly Father." I was quite surprised to find that the desire for life continues even until the actual beckoning call of death.

What does this mean for the patient? In our situation, my father continued to learn and thirst for new knowledge. During the last months of his life, he bought second-hand German records at a library rummage sale so he could refresh his language skills. When he had the strength, he looked up definitions of words to work on crossword puzzles. Not until his last morning, when he essentially asked my permission to die, did he give up that thirst for life. And from what I've discovered from others, his was not an unusual situation. If nothing else in this book applies to your situation, this insight should be a constant in your caregiving. It might help you understand what your loved one is feeling. And even though discouragements come and depression may lead to, "I just want to die," remember that what the patient really wants is to *live*. My husband, John, says he is not afraid of death; it's dying that he dislikes. Life is a precious gift that is hard to understand. Although Christians live in another dimension when it comes to life and death, God still created us to live here on earth as physical beings.

Dignity and Worth

Understanding life will affect the way we understand and treat our loved one who is facing the inevitable loss of this gift. Kris Hollingbery, a geriatric nurse and instructor in Yakima, Washington, says "Every person has value and worth. Dignity should be maintained through to death. The caregiver should know that treating the patient in this manner comes out of one's love for him or her, because this person is God's creation."

Hollingbery also stresses that one of the most important things a caregiver can remember—and she teaches this to geriatric students—is that the caregiver should acknowledge a person's dignity and worth from the very beginning of the caregiving. He or she should create a bonding that shows appreciation for the person as a contributing part of society, up until the very end of life. Hollingbery suggests that the caregiver, whether a family member or a professional, can accomplish this by asking things like "What were you like as a child? How did you earn your living?" and other questions that give the caregiver insights into the patient's life.

It is also important for the caregiver, particularly those who are professionals, to know from the beginning that, if the person is terminally ill, one must look emotionally toward the end of the patient's life, according to Hollingbery. You must understand the patient is dying; for the time will come when you must detach yourself and let him or her go. How one does this is an individual matter. The message here is to love, care for, and treat with great dignity, but also to continue throughout the caregiving, "letting that person go with respect," and not clinging after life and being emotionally bound to them.

For caregivers of the elderly and dying, the experts all agree: Not only acknowledge the person's dignity and self-worth, but also try to understand the aging process. "I think that caregivers should have a knowledge of elderly issues and the process of aging. For instance, older people go back to things in life, recall old events in their lives in ways that we may think are bizarre, but they are still processing things. The caregiver needs to see the elderly as vital, active, alive, energetic people, and they need to maintain dignity up to death," says Dr. Ron Shackleford, a pastor and founder/owner of a board and care facility.

Gerontologist Alana Peters agrees, "Understand the aging process. Don't blame [idiosyncracies] on getting old. Age exacerbates all you've been dealing with all of your life. If you're cranky, it's not because you're old. It's because you've always been cranky. Old people don't get cranky; cranky people get old." In fact, many people die bitter and angry, often misunderstood by the ones who love them the most.

Be an Advocate for the Patient

"Be vigilant as an advocate for the patient and expedite their resources to meet their needs. This means knowing about the patient's medications, financial resources, and family and spiritual resources," says Elizabeth Brown, a geriatric nursing instructor and specialist. What she says here reaffirms the total caregiving experience. You become the eyes, ears, and feet for the patient, the one who must oversee the total care.

You Are Not Alone

I wish I had known that when I first became a caregiver. But I thought I could do it myself with the help of the doctors and my immediate and extended family. What I didn't know was that things would snowball, and by the time I realized there were resources available, it was too late to incorporate many of them into my life without major changes and possible misunderstanding on my father's part. The lack of time and the stresses of the urgent needs did not allow time to even think about getting help. Hollingbery suggests that one of the most important things a caregiver can do is to always know the available backup resources. Know the telephone numbers and the people to contact for various helps. She adds, "Don't make a unilateral decision without using the experience of others."

Isolation—being cooped up at home for days and weeks while getting out of the house only for necessary shopping and doctor's appointments—gives the caregiver the feeling that "I am alone. I'm the only person who has ever experienced this. People just don't know what it's like. No one else can possibly understand." This is far from the truth, and things are changing with the surge in interest and the media attention about the plight of caregivers, as well as the formation of many new support groups.

Immediately examine the resources that are available, before time passes. Of course, the patient is your number one concern, that is understood. But if the caregiver does not have some resources upon which to call when the time is right and when they are necessary, then the walls of isolation will be almost impenetrable. I will never forget the afternoon when the home care nurse first came to our home (at the request of the oncologist) to introduce herself to my father and me. We were not emotionally prepared for her visit, and we did not think we needed her. Yet she was very understanding and gracious, and talked about the things that she could provide for us. We denied to ourselves that we would ever need her help. Besides, my father was still hoping, in God's sovereignty, to get better and be healed, even though he had faced the fact that his cancer was terminal.

Thankfully, when we did reach the point of needing help, we already had the knowledge of those home care services. We had a name and a face. It was a relief to know that help existed (self-administered pain medications; oxygen that could be set up at home; help for personal hygiene—bathing, and so on). All I had to do was open the file the nurse had left with us, read the information, and activate the service.

Time for Yourself Must Be Planned

Make time for yourself, even from the earliest days of your caregiving. This may sound selfish to you; it certainly did to me. In fact, I almost resented hearing it. Didn't people know it was my *father* who was dying? I was strong and well, but they acted as if I needed the help. I wanted them to be more concerned for him than for me. I felt the need to sacrifice for him, since he had sacrificed for me throughout my lifetime. It was my way to show him my love. And that's valid reasoning. My father's care was my primary concern. He was dying. How could I possibly think of myself?

As the saying goes, hindsight is better than foresight. I needed to listen to others because they cared for me as well as for my father. By the time I realized this, however, it was too far down the road to make many changes. I've paid for the fact that I did not plan a few hours each week for my own health and welfare. My body became run-down and, as a result, I contracted many infections and small ailments.

More and more is being said by health care professionals—those who deal with caregivers—and by caregivers themselves about the need for caregivers to take care. If this is not done, the cycle of responsibility for another's care will become not only the most important thing in your life, but also the only thing. It is very demanding—and the patient, no matter how understanding he or she may be, is too ill and preoccupied with the daily functions of living to realize what is happening to you.

How can the caregiver plan to find time for himself or herself? I suggest that at the very beginning of your caregiving you gently let the patient know that you have certain responsibilities of your own. You can either talk with the patient about this without letting him feel he is being a burden, or you can simply establish your own schedule without discussion. To be sure, you must flex your schedule to fit with the patient's changing daily needs. But you can still do things like exercise regularly. Find someone to "spell" you at night, even just once or twice a week, to begin with. And you can plan a regular time away from the house.

This may sound very self-centered, and you may resent what I am saying, particularly if you are just beginning your caregiving. But you need to set a pattern of help early, so that you can still function at your physical, emotional, and psychological best toward the end of your caregiving time. By then you will already be on a schedule to take care of yourself. And it's also important to find those with whom you can be yourself, with whom you can laugh and let down a little bit, and with whom you can pray.

Respite Care

Respite care is available in many communities, particularly for the caregivers of Alzheimer's patients. Throughout the country many churches and adult day-care centers are being formed where the patient can be dropped off for a day of rest for the caregiver. Many have family, friends, or church members who are willing to come in for a few hours each week. Many times a caregiver hesitates to call an adult day-care center, feeling that they might be letting down on the job. It is important to explore this kind of care and to take advantage of it. You will be very grateful for those few hours a week to have a little bit of time to catch your breath.

Use Common Sense

In the caregiving situation, use the same type of common sense that you would use in raising children (for the average parent, that is!). You will find that nine out of ten times you will make the right decisions.

Begin a Regular, Festive, Special Time

The week following my husband's heart attack and after he had stabilized but was still hospitalized, our two adult children and I, and the friend who had administered CPR, began such a pattern of activity. Every day we left the hospital for about an hour to eat dinner at a nearby restaurant. To the observer it may have seemed a very self-centered, frivolous thing to do. But it turned out to be just what we needed—an upbeat time where our stress, emotions, and deep concerns could be shared together, along with the luxury of being served a meal in a relaxed, quiet setting. This need for a positive, special time and setting continued when John came home to recuperate. Only instead of eating in restaurants we ate our meals with candlelight and flowers, and we rented videos that were positive and fun. The release of stress in a nonthreatening, nondemanding, relaxed atmosphere and a short time with a change of environment are primary needs for the caregiver's emotional and psychological well-being. (And the patient's too!)

Take Notes

Write *everything* down in your Caregiver's Manual.

I don't care how good your memory is, how busy you are, or what the circumstances are—take notes. Buy a thick spiral notebook that you can carry with you, one that will last for a long time. Begin writing everything down: what the doctor says, a description of the patient's moods and comments, who comes to visit, medications, procedures, and so forth. Make this notebook your Caregiver's Log. Hollingbery says, "It is very beneficial for the continuity of patient care to keep such a diary—from a nursing standpoint, it is very helpful."

Sample Caregiver's Manual:

date	time	medica-tion	blood pressure	temper-ature	food intake	com-ment	food	initial
10/5	8:04 A.M.	Roxanol, 2cc	104/70	99.6		bad pain	prunes, hot tea w. sugar	cmd
	10:15 A.M.						straw-berry shake	jmd

Notes: "Radiation seems to be affecting esophagus and swallowing. Called Dr. T.

Note taking can be combined with a daily schedule and log of medications, blood pressure and temperature readings, food intake, and other important medical information (i.e., regularity; enemas; pains; color of the skin; nutritional intake, noting changes in the amount (decrease or increase) for a twenty-four hour period; telephone conversations with doctors and nurses; blood tests and other test results; helpful information from health care professionals; etc.) This log will serve you well when you need to reconstruct a pattern of care or report to the doctor or nurse in the future.

Another important reason for such a daily diary: When another person must take over in either caregiving or administering medication, it's necessary to have all the information in one place. Granted, there is the patient's hospital/doctor's chart. But the chart takes hours to review for medications and changes, test results, and previous instructions. The primary caregiver really needs to know, understand, and be the coordinator of this information. In the event of several persons giving care, this log is vital to the uninterrupted flow of care for the patient.

My three sisters and I, as well as uncles, aunts, and grandchildren, all took turns caring for Daddy. This log was particularly helpful when my father underwent chemotherapy and was still living in his Florida home. It was our practice to write out instructions for the next shift since we each spent at least one week with him over a three-month period of time. This detailed log gave continuity. We noted such practical things as where to buy Ensure food supplement at the best prices, particular sanitization needs (dishes sterilized), and so on. We even had set time limits for visitors, as per our father's request.

Another example of the usefulness of the Caregiver's Log occurred during the same time my father underwent chemotherapy. Since the strong chemicals affected his heart adversely, he had to be hospitalized over a weekend for heart monitoring before continuing the treatment. His primary doctors were on vacation, and all the regular on-call doctors were away. Thus the doctors who attended my father were pulled from other practices or from the hospital staff itself. They had no knowledge of his condition, his medical background, or his particular needs. I'm certain they were good doctors. But had my sister not been with my father, along with the log of medications, recent medical history, and data pertinent to his condition, unnecessary tests would have been run, and he would have been hospitalized longer than necessary. He was in no condition to speak for himself and tell the doctor the sequence of past medical occurrences.

Maintaining Strength and Equilibrium

Every day spent in a hospital brings the terminally ill or weakened patient down a bit—not only psychologically, but also physically. The confinement to bed for tests and EKG hookups debilitates. When life is on the edge, a patient can physically deteriorate quickly during some of the therapy treatments. Even though the patient may be terminally ill, the longer he or she can maintain strength and independence, even at a low energy level, both psychologically and physically, the stronger the patient will be up to the end of his or her life. And the easier the caregiving situation will become.

Medications, the illness itself, depression, and other psychological distresses may affect the patient's moods. The caregiver must be aware that some medications cause personality and mood swings and changes. These need to be checked out with the pharmacist (often easier to reach than the doctor) and reported to the doctor if they persist, even for a day or two. One sleeping pill was affecting my father's moods. He was not himself; he knew it, and I certainly could tell. With a couple of telephone calls, we were able to adjust the medication and try something else.

Pain affects moods and can cause swings in personality. The patient can tolerate more pain at some times than at others. For instance, pain seems to be more difficult to deal with at night because the patient is tired and things are quiet. There are fewer distractions. And yet, if the pain is there, but the patient is not totally aware of it, this can make the patient so uncomfortable that he or she reacts in a negative way.

You know your patient. He or she may have been a complainer or talked about medical problems before the illness. You may have disregarded their complaints, their focus on themselves, and their medical problems. Now, however, is the time to change your attitude toward that person. Listen to his or her concerns, and don't be afraid to call the doctor or the doctor's nurse or assistant. Take every complaint seriously. Don't just tolerate the complaint; try to discover what the real need is. And, if indeed the patient is just in need of attention, by all means find ways to give it to him or her. If you can't handle it—and most people say it does get tiresome after a while—then find someone to give you a break.

What about Medications?

Particular caution must be taken with medications given to older patients, who make up the majority of caregiving situations. Recent research has shown that the older person reacts to drugs in much different ways than do the young. In an article written by Jane E. Brody for *The New York Times,* an example is given of an older woman who took a certain drug for thirty months before she realized that the many physical problems she was experiencing—loss of balance and memory, depression, unease and lassitude, among others—were affected by one medication. After a serious fall, she stopped taking her medications one by one and identified this drug. Within forty-eight hours after she stopped taking the drug, she began feeling normal. She discovered that the particular drug was listed with a warning in a book on medicines older people should avoid. The warning said: Do Not Use."[1] It also warned of special mental and physical adverse effects.[2]

Brian S. Katcher, a doctor of pharmacology in San Francisco, said one major hospital study showed that people over sixty were fifteen times more likely than younger patients to be admitted to a hospital for drug-induced illnesses.[3] He also warned that elderly patients are more susceptible to ill effects from drug interactions, where one drug will cancel out the effect of another, or will have an adverse effect. This was certainly true in my father's experience, and many others have said the same thing. He took a drug for one condition, and he ended up taking another drug to compensate for the problems associated with the first one. And so on. The news media frequently focuses on new medical information about drugs. The caregiver must take that data and confer with the physician to double check that the medication is being properly administered.

Many in the health care profession echo the findings of recent research: "Not only do older people often take more drugs and more combinations of drugs than younger people, but other physical factors tend to make drug reaction different for the older patient. The brain and other organs grow more sensitive, leading to over-sedation or unstable blood pressure and dizziness. Water soluble drugs may become more concentrated in older people whose blood and water volume decreases. Fat-soluble drugs may accumulate and cause long-lasting delayed effects, also because of changed body composition. Kidney and liver function may decline with age, so that the body metabolizes and excretes drugs less efficiently. Psychological factors may make drug problems look like signs of aging, and older people may fail to follow directions."[4]

The facts described here can become only more complex for the terminally or chronically ill older patient. The caregiver is the one who must pay attention and oversee what the patient takes, particularly if there is more than one doctor involved in the patient's care. Even though doctors communicate with each other, it is almost impossible for them to keep abreast of all the various medications. In the event that the communication was not current, I used my log of medications to update the various doctors—oncologist, radiation oncologist, pulmonary specialist, and any on-call or backup doctors or those specialists who were called in for various problems, such as a cardiologist or a gastroenterologist.

"Many physicians do not realize that the elderly are more susceptible to adverse reactions and thus fail to make needed adjustments in dosages or to monitor older patients for ill effects,"[5] said Helene Lipton and Philip Lee, researchers at the University of California, San Francisco. "One common symptom, drug-induced dementia, is often dismissed as a sign of old age instead of being recognized as a reversible toxic effect."[6] For the caregiver of the elderly, this kind of behavior by the patient is often the most difficult to see and handle, yet it is possible that in many cases the patient may be taking drugs that are causing these side effects.

Caregivers need to be as informed as possible, keep detailed records, ask questions of both doctors and pharmacists, and be certain that the patient follows the instructions given for taking each drug.

Post a List of Telephone Numbers

List telephone numbers by each telephone and know when to call the doctor, nurse, 911, neighbors, pastor, church prayer chain, or family members. Also keep a list of these numbers in your purse or wallet so you will have it wherever you go.

Put Together an Emergency Kit

Keep it in your purse or carry it along with you for unexpected trips to the emergency room, the doctor, or a ride in the car. Take extra medication, the phone list, and extra cash. To this day I hide a $20 bill from myself and then forget about it, in case I end up in the emergency room or a hospital room and have had no time to go to the bank. This cash at least allows me to buy food or gasoline, should I need either. I also used to take a granola bar for myself, crackers or cookies and small cans of juice for my father, a blowup travel neck pillow for the car, a pad and pencil in addition to my Caregiver's Log. I always carried my father's Social Security number, his Medicare and other insurance cards, and driver's license. And, of course, the handicapped sticker always went in my purse.

Pain Is Often Manageable

One of the biggest fears of the future for both the patient and the caregiver is "Will there be much pain?" We were advised early on in the illness that my father would probably be able to control his pain, particularly toward the end of his life. There are drugs and combinations of drugs that can take care of that, in most cases. In my father's case as with other patients, however, he put off taking much medication for the time he would need it. I believe now he suffered a lot more than was necessary, at least up until near the end of his life. Most of the time his pain tolerance level was much higher than an average person's. Finding that tolerance level of pain is an individual matter. Sometimes patients choose to have some pain rather than to be under the possible drugging effects of the medication. Nevertheless, it is important to take care of the *edge* of the pain. There is no need to suffer when help is available. Many people have been able to take morphine, for instance, and still function quite well with only periodic naps. The times when the pain is under good control are the times that are most enjoyable for both caregiver and, obviously, the patient.

The caregiver should be aware of the possibility that the patient is not receiving enough pain medication. "The vast majority [of the world's cancer patients] are undermedicated for their pain," according to the World Health Organization studies.[7] Yet it needn't be that way, according to many doctors. Doctors usually start on a pain management approach, beginning with aspirin and acetaminophen, then a mild narcotic with codeine, an opium-based morphine, and then, in many cases, a concoction such as the "Brompton's cocktail," or other such combination (ingredients vary from place to place, but most commonly include: a narcotic, a stimulant, an antiemetic — a substance to counteract nausea and vomiting — and a flavoring agent, such as cherry syrup).

Naturally, the question is asked, "Why do people suffer when there is help to relieve the pain?" One reason is that "many physicians are not trained to deal with pain. Until recently, medical school curricula rarely included lectures in pain control, and the subject was barely mentioned in textbooks. Many patients suffer simply because caregivers are not familiar with current thinking in regard to the aggressive treatment of pain."[8]

Many doctors now adhere to pain prevention, prescribing medication on a regular schedule whether or not the patient asks for it. Since this is such an individual matter, I would strongly suggest that the caregiver be certain that the patient investigates pain prevention and the effects of various drugs. Do not let the patient suffer needlessly. Be aware that in some states drugs such as morphine are monitored closely by the state. Thus some doctors do not prescribe the amount of medication that a patient might need. Check out all of the options.

Addiction to the pain medication is a major concern for many patients. "Addiction probably occurs in less than one percent of persons who take narcotics for pain relief. Addiction is usually defined as the regular use of narcotics for emotional or psychic reasons, rather than for medical reasons. Pain relief is a medical reason for taking narcotics. Therefore, if you are taking narcotics to relieve your pain, you are not an addict no matter how much or how often you take narcotics."[9]

At this time in a terminally ill patient's life, he or she should not be worried about addiction. It seems a senseless concern. Lest the patient be unwilling to face his or her own mortality, it is up to the caregiver to help them understand that possible addiction is really a moot question.

Another common fear for the patient is that pain medication will make them too drowsy to be alert. In many situations this is not the case after a few days on the narcotic. Sometimes the pain relief actually allows the patient to catch up on much-needed sleep. And sometimes other medications the patient is taking may be causing the drowsiness. If extreme drowsiness occurs, call the doctor or nurse. And keep good records of the patient's pain and its control. "Until recently it was thought that increasing the dose of strong narcotics such as morphine and methadone would increase serious side effects without adding to pain relief. However, with careful medical observation, the doses of strong narcotics (by mouth or injection) can be safely raised to high levels so that severe pain can be eased. If the pain is not relieved and the doctor does not seem to be aware of other alternatives, ask for a consultation with a pain specialist."[10]

Depression and Sleep Deprivation

Depression is very common in home or hospital-bound patients, but it is treatable. Oftentimes it does not take much to help a depressed person—it can be as simple as correcting a chemical imbalance or a nutritional deficiency. The caregiver should be aware of this and the fact that there is help. Check with your doctor, nurse, or a licensed social or mental health worker. *Sleep deprivation* sometimes accompanies the depression and may be occurring if the patient is also experiencing pain. The patient may be grieving and just need to spend some time talking about what is going on inside. If sleep deprivation is occurring and just talking about it does not help the situation, a change in pain medication could be necessary. You may see a remarkable change in attitude if pain is under control. And for a short time, the patient might sleep more during the daytime, catching up on much-needed rest.

Keep Current on Insurance Forms and Doctors' Billings

This is much easier said than done. I was totally unprepared for the world of insurance forms, doctors' billings, Medicare, and supplementary insurance, and the way they work. In general, I was not ready for the business aspects of the patient's care. First, I suggest that the caregiver organize a place to keep everything. Use file folders for each category of business — hospitals, doctors, laboratory, special testing (CAT scan, x-ray, MRI, etc.) — and keep copies of the bills filed separately until the insurance has paid for them. There are so many different aspects to the insurance morass that for the uninitiated it can be quite overwhelming. If there is someone in your family who thrives on this kind of detail, or someone who can take care of it for you, by all means let them do it. It is important, however, for the primary caregiver to know just what is happening, to be certain there are no "surprises" at a doctor's office and with a bill that may have been overlooked and unpaid.

Find out what insurance policies the patient has and, for the older patient, which doctors accept "assignment" for Medicare. Often doctors who do not take assignment may waive the extra cost if you talk with them about this. The insurance and health care business is so complex, there are so many variables, and change happens so frequently, that I can only say the caregiver *must* keep up. Don't get behind, or it will be a monumental task to sort it all out. Ask questions, and find help. There are agencies, and sometimes support groups, community groups, or health care professionals who can steer you to the needed help. In many hospitals there are staff people to assist the patient in understanding how to plan ahead. Don't give up. Be as informed as you possibly can be. And do it right away.

Often the laboratory or some doctors use billing firms to keep their accounts for them. These names will appear on Medicare forms and will need to be identified. This may mean calling the Medicare or other insurance offices. Don't be afraid to question a Medicare or other insurance payment—oftentimes it is a simple matter to clear up. At the present time, a provider handles Medicare in each state. If the patient must move from one state to another, the caregiver will need to keep track of the bills and payments from each state provider during the transition. Otherwise, you may have a bill pop up months later, long forgotten. It will probably be difficult to remember even what it was for, so much may have happened during the interim.

Plan Ahead for Blood Transfusions

This is certainly something you should discuss with your physician. The blood supply system has greatly improved during the past few years, following a rash of AIDS cases and deaths caused by tainted blood supply. This is often a nagging concern, even for the dying patient. Nevertheless, it is a good idea in some situations to have blood donated for the patient, in the event it may be needed and particularly for those cancer patients who have some hope for palliative care for a time. Sources may be found in your church (some churches have a blood bank for their congregation) or family and friends. It is a precautionary step that could be planned for in the event that it is needed.

Buy a Book on Home Nursing

Find some tips for caring for the patient that can be easily read and applied, either at home, in a nursing home, hospice, or hospital. Some simple things to be learned include how to give back and neck rubs, administering enemas, changing beds, sanitation precautions, things to look for in the patient's overall health, and so on.

Common abbreviations for prescriptions include:

'c = with
prn = as needed

cc = cubic centimeter
ml = milliliter (1 ml = 1 cc)
gm = gram (1 gm = 1000 mg)
mg = milligram (60–64 mg = a gr)
gr = grain (measure of weight)
po = by mouth, orally
pr = per rectum
# = number, usually the number of tablets pre-scribed and dispensed
q = every
qd = every day
qod = every other day
bid = two times a day
tid = three times a day
qid = four times a day

Example: *#30 Tylenol 'c Cod 1/2 gr q 4 h prn for pain. This means "30 Tylenol tablets with 1/2 grain of Codeine in each tablet. You can take a tablet no more often than every four hours if needed for pain relief."* [11]

There is a lot to know and a lot to remember. Above all, remember that the patient, whether young or old, with a short-term or terminal illness, is the reason for giving care. You give this care because of the love that comes from God.

The expectations for quality care can be met with good common sense. A sense of humor and a dose of joy will go a long way toward building confidence and teamwork—for both the caregiver and the patient.

Medical Terminology

The terms that follow are just a few of the common terminology that you may need to learn as a caregiver. These are defined in popular terminology; you may want to check with your doctor, nurse, or pharmacist for verification of the terms you are dealing with in your own particular situation.

ADL	Activities of daily living—a measurement of what a patient can or cannot do for him or herself (from washing one's face to grocery shopping)
Antiemetic	Medication given to stop nausea
Ascites	Ascites—fluid accumulates in the abdomen, causing swelling
Cardiac	Matters related to the heart
Catheters	Means tubing used for draining fluid from or injecting fluid into the body. Some types are: Foley's (for urination), suction (used orally), super pubic, rectal, naso-gastric, PEG (gastrostomy—for food), percutaneous (endo-gastrostomy)
CAT scanning	Computerized scanning of the body, known as CT scanning
Chemotherapy	The treatment of disease (cancer) by the use of chemical agents; can be administered orally or intravenously
Constipation	Inability to have a bowel movement or the stool is hard and difficult to evacuate
Diarrhea	Liquid and frequent bowel movements
Dressing	Bandages
Edema	Usually where fluid accumulates and causes swelling of the extremities
Effusion	Fluid escapes through the walls of a blood vessel into a body cavity
Electrolytes	Ions that have an important role in regulating the body functions, such as potassium, hydrogen, calcium, magnesium, sodium, chloride, bicarbonate, phosphate
Hematocrit (Hct)	The percentage of red blood cells

per volume of whole blood

Hemoglobin (Hbg)
A special component of blood cells that carries oxygen and carbon dioxide

Hyperalimentation
A chemical mix of nutrients and electrolytes to be put back into the body to sustain life; for patients unable to take food by mouth

Incontinence
Uncontrollable, involuntary urination or inability to retain feces in the rectum

Lines
Used when referring to drawing blood or administering liquids into the body: *Intravenous* (IV) — within a vein — an IV infusion is the slow introduction of fluid into the blood stream, also known as a *drip*. The IV usually refers to the peripheral parts of the body. A *central* line refers to a major vein in a more central part of the body, not on the peripheral parts. *Central access implantable receptacle* — a permanent access for administration of medications, fluids, or the drawing of blood. Provides easy access when the peripheral veins are weakened. (A port is an example of this kind of central access receptacle.) The term "access" is used when using a permanent receptacle. A PCA pump is used by the patient to self-administer medications, usually pain medication.

MRI
Magnetic resonance imaging, a diagnostic technique that provides cross-sectional images of the organs and body structure without x-

	rays or radiation
Nasal canula	Tube inserted into the nostrils to provide oxygen
Nasogastric tube	Narrow tube that is inserted through the nose, esophagus, and into the stomach, to either drain digestive juices from the stomach when there is an intestinal blockage, or it is used to give liquid nourishment to very ill patients who cannot eat
Neutraponia	A decrease in white blood cells
Oncology	The study of tumors (cancers)
Pain management	Caring for the patient's pain by various methods, including preventative scheduling of medication, relaxation and other techniques
Palliative	To keep comfortable — moderate the intensity of the disease and pain; includes using stress management and the management of pain to control and make the physical suffering more bearable
Radiation therapy	The treatment of disease by the use of ionizing radiation
Red blood cells (RBC)	Component of blood; carry oxygen to the tissue and carbon dioxide from the tissue
Renal	Related to the kidney — renal failure is sometimes called uremia
Respiratory system	Provides energy needed by the body cells — the process by which oxygen reaches the body's cells, is utilized for metabolism, and through which carbon dioxide is eliminated from the body.
Urinalysis	Tests taken on a person's urine to check a variety of body functions, in-

cluding the kidney and urinary tract, etc.

White blood cells (WBC)

Component of blood; main function is to fight infection

CHAPTER FOUR
Planning Ahead

Planning ahead for caregiving is almost a contradiction in terms. How can one possibly plan ahead? You are probably already in the middle of a caregiving situation if you're reading this. If that is the case, take heart. There are some things that you can still plan ahead for, and you will need to enlist your family's help in most situations. "I feel that the number one concern for the caregiver is learning to plan ahead, not wait for a crisis," said Alana Peters, gerontologist. "If possible, sit down and make out a preparedness list: 'What will we do if . . . ' 'Where will we live if . . .' If you are already in the middle of the caregiving situation, keep planning for the next step. And keep your sense of humor. Find something to laugh at together.'"[1] This advice is true for caregivers of both the young and the old.

If you are a potential caregiver of an older relative, this chapter will be of even greater benefit to you. When planning for your parents' or spouse's—or even your own—later years and the eventuality of being either bedridden or dependent on others, you will want to get your own life in such order that you and those who will possibly be your caregivers will receive adequate care. The following suggestions focus primarily on the elderly, but many of the principles can be used with younger patients as well.

Be Realistic about Your Commitment to Caregiving

One of the most important things to tell caregivers of the elderly, right at the very beginning, is to be certain that "when you make a commitment to take the caregiving duties, also make a commitment to the time when you will no longer be able to give care," says Elizabeth Brown. "In other words, set your limits, and plan for the time when you will need to give up the caregiving, whether it means placing the patient in a full-care facility or providing for other options that the patient may need, such as hospice, hospital, etc.

"The caregiving is only going to get more complex as the days progress. You will particularly lose ground with the elderly as they lose their ability to control their bodily functions and their self-sufficiency. And in the case of Alzheimer's or senile dementia, they will also lose their ability to relate to you personally. Ask the question: 'At what point can you no longer give care?' Most caregivers often only look at the moment. As a caregiver you need to know your turn-off points, you need to know at what place in the caregiving you can go no further, and plan for that eventuality and what you will need to do at that time, i.e., nursing home, extra help in the home, etc."

Be Prepared

Planning ahead is crucial — this cannot be stressed enough. If at first you don't understand a lot of the many new details — the jargon, terminology, processes of filing, and needs for clarification — don't give up. Keep asking questions. And try to find an agency or expert that can help you sort through this seeming morass. In California a non-profit organization called HICAP (Health Insurance Counseling and Advocacy Program) is funded by a grant from the California Department of Aging and is sponsored by the Visiting Nurses Association Foundation. This organization is 95 percent staffed by volunteers, and it provides education counseling regarding Medicare supplemental policies. It helps alleviate some of the confusion associated with filing forms, errors in processing claims, and advertisements for supplemental insurance policies or medigap policies. It also helps set up a record-keeping form for claims. It offers referrals for legal representatives, if necessary, and explains long-term insurance. Personnel will address clubs and organizations on the subject and the organization's function. This program has already saved the state of California and seniors thousands of dollars in claims and legal advice.[2] Such a program in your state can be a valuable resource to you.

Planning ahead is easier to say than to do. Whether the person you are caring for is old or young, he or she may not be able to face the future. That person either may be in denial of the situation and thinks he or she is and will be capable of handling the financial and legal affairs, or may be too sick to think about it. In any case, you must persist and press on to accomplish adequate care for his or her well-being. There are several ways to do this, and hopefully it will be easy for you.

First, I urge you and someone you trust (possibly a "prayer partner") to spend time in concerted prayer as you oversee this important part of your caregiving responsibilities. Knowing that you have prayer and moral support will encourage you. I believe God is interested in and cares about these difficult decisions.

Second, prepare a "pre-plan" so you know what needs to be done to get things in order. The areas listed in this chapter should give you some guidance as to what is necessary. Ask yourself questions like, "What do I need to know in order to make good decisions?" "What do I need to do?" "Who else needs to be a part of the decision-making?" "Is there someone else in the family who is better qualified than I to take care of all these details?" Ideally, the patient should agree to this planning process, but you also need to think about the dynamics of your family and be certain that they all agree to and understand what you plan to do. If you are the primary caregiver, the responsibility really falls on your shoulders to get the ball rolling!

Third, try to get the approval from the older patient to plan for his or her future days. If this is agreeable, it will be much easier. But you will probably still need to formulate a plan for things to be decided.

Fourth, when you have a plan in mind, and some kind of support either from the patient, family members (your spouse, siblings, or children, as the case may be), or an outside person you can trust to help you think clearly, sit down with the patient and present your plan. Remember, you must consider the well-being of the patient; this is your number one concern. If the patient is unwilling to cooperate, gently encourage him or her to understand the necessity of having things in order. Be patient, understanding, and loving, but be persistent. You will be thankful in later days if you can accomplish this early in caregiving.

My husband, John, was called to his mother's bedside as she was near death. We didn't know she was as ill as she was, because she had been doing well on her own in her own home. But when a call came from the hospital during the early morning hours saying she was in intensive care with both a stroke and advancing cancer, we were totally unprepared. We were still fairly young (in our mid-forties) and were completely unaware of the need to plan ahead for such emergencies. We had tried, unsuccessfully, for a number of years to get her to move closer to us, but she insisted on staying in her small Florida home near her church, friends, neighbors, and sister.

When John arrived at the hospital, it was necessary for him to make life-and-death decisions. He had to get his mother to sign a "Power of Attorney" document in order to make arrangements for her care. To this day, many years later, it still bothers him to have had his mother sign such a document in her terribly weak condition, so close to her imminent death. We could have avoided such pain, for her and for John, had we known what to do with a plan of action for such an eventuality.

In another situation an elderly friend has been hospitalized in the full-care facility of his retirement home with cancer and heart problems. His situation is terminal, and his condition is deteriorating daily. A widower, he was recently remarried, and his wife is at his bedside caring for him daily. She is God's provision for his needs for companionship and love during his last days since his children are far away. The only problem is that his children (and his new wife) do not have power of attorney for him in order to make necessary business decisions. Their hands are virtually tied from attending to his well-being. The trauma of obtaining such power, even for necessary medical care, is emotionally too difficult at present for both husband and wife. In addition, the adult children have great difficulty in taking care of minor financial concerns, such as selling his car and disposing of furniture.

Family Meeting

It is much easier to plan ahead while you and the potential patient are not in need of care. Hold a family meeting for the whole family, in order to include everyone. This way there will be no questions in the future, particularly from those who live away from the patient. "The rule is, 'the earlier the better' when planning for health and financial arrangements. Serious medical problems without any prior planning generally give the patient, the primary caregiver and the family a one-two blow. The first blow is the emotional upheaval at the onset of the problem. This is quickly followed by blow two, the overwhelming financial burden that soon follows and has no answers and no end."[3]

The plan needs to contain information on the patient's (or potential patient's) health care benefits (insurance policies, Medicare, etc.) and all sources of income which include potential future income and other sources of support, such as from inheritance and family. "Read every insurance policy carefully and get help from an agent or professional organization to help with your questions, such as 'What happens when they become sick? When they become disabled?' "[4]

Many former caregivers say the same thing: We ran out of resources, both Medicare and personal resources, and it was a difficult situation. Life savings were eaten up in a short amount of time. "In our situation," according to Marjorie Stiles, who helped her father care for her aging mother before she was placed in a nursing home, "the finances were difficult to face, because Medicare only covers about five months of the nursing home care. That means that each year there were about seven months of care without insurance." This is a very real problem and a very complex one. But it must be sorted through for the benefit of all concerned.

This planning session can be difficult as well, but if all parties realize its importance, it can bring tremendous relief, particularly to the patient. I would urge you to include a time of prayer together as a family, since this will focus on the Lord, who is the Source of life, and indeed on the many blessings given throughout one's life. I truly believe God is interested in the little and big decisions that we make, and that families must continue to seek God's guidance for such difficult and mundane, yet important, matters as these.

Financial Situation

"An efficient financial presentation in writing enables everyone in the family to review the true financial picture, unemotionally, and determine if any additional investments need to be made. Look for duplications in benefits and extra [insurance] premiums that may not be necessary."[5] These words should be of comfort to many people facing their own future needs. The laws and health care situation in the United States are changing, hopefully soon for the better.

Insurance, Medicare, and Medicaid

Long-term care for the young and old is a financial drain, no matter what the circumstances. It is crucial that parents, caring for a child or young person, find ways to manage this burden in order to maintain stability. Communication with health care providers, hospitals, doctors, and insurance companies is critical in order to get through this crisis.

For the terminally ill older patient it is important to look at the Social Security benefits. Medicare and Supplementary Social Security (SSI) benefits need to be considered as well. These can be discussed with the Social Security office. Be sure to ask what the long-term possibilities are with your benefits, that is, nursing home coverage, and so on.

A brief overview of Medicare may be helpful. Medicare is federally funded and is administered by the Social Security Administration for persons sixty-five years of age and older. Medicare has two parts: Part A and Part B. Medicare Parts A and B can be purchased together, or only Part B can be purchased. Part A cannot be purchased separately.

Part A pays for some of the hospital bills: inpatient hospital care, medically necessary inpatient care in a skilled nursing facility, home health care, and hospice care. A Medigap or supplemental insurance will help cover the remaining expenses.

Part B helps pay for doctors' services, outpatient hospital care, diagnostic tests, durable medical equipment, ambulance services, and supplies not covered by Part A. Supplemental insurance will often help cover the remainder of the expenses, either part or all of Medicare's copayments and deductibles. A Medigap policy must be labeled "Medicare Supplemental Coverage." Since some procedures are not covered, the caregiver should check with the Medicare office. Be certain to see how many days are covered in a full-care facility or nursing home, and what the stipulations are in your situation. In many cases, insurance does not cover the necessary bills, and you should know exactly what will be covered.

Be certain that the doctors accept "assignment" for the amount (the standard fees) that Medicare will pay. It is important to keep up with the amounts that are being charged the patient and the amount that Medicare is paying.

Don't be afraid to question a Medicare payment. They do make mistakes, and they are willing to make adjustments. But it may take some effort on your part.

Since Medicaid, also a part of the Social Security Act, is both federally and state funded, the amount of benefits varies with each state. It assists needy patients, and it can be contacted through either the local state's Department of Welfare or the Department of Social Services. When the patient's Medicare allotment and personal finances are depleted, Medicaid pays for certain things, but the choices of facilities are often limited. Therefore, check out these potential resources. Several caregivers of the elderly have expressed their frustrations that the depletion of Medicare and personal resources left their family with no alternatives for care.

The reassurance to all concerned that you are merely planning ahead and have the well-being and the best interests of the patient in mind will relieve a lot of difficulties and questions. If this is done well ahead of the need while the person is only a potential patient or in the early stages of care, you will help the older person realize he or she may be supported in their own home as long as possible.

Elder Law is a growing specialty that focuses on the elderly and their particular needs, and those involved in this specialty can be very helpful to the caregiver, patient, and family. Not only does this area of legal services address the issues of estate-planning, but it also covers setting up a durable power of attorney for health care and the living trust to protect one's resources from probate and taxes. Lawyers specializing in elder legal issues can be obtained through community resources, as well as through the National Academy of Elder Law Attorneys, Inc.[6]

Durable Power of Attorney

The Durable Power of Attorney gives a person the right to make all decisions for another person. It can be rescinded, however, by simply signing a document stating such wishes. Indeed, this one document has brought considerable controversy in the media in recent years. It seems to cause fear because this means the person is in a position to lose control. The possible abuses, of course, should be considered. But the flip side of having such a document is also important to consider. There is a high degree of trust given to the person to whom Power of Attorney is assigned. For the Christian this should make perfect sense. We should be able to trust our lives to ones in our family who are trustworthy and loved and whom we know love us. Unfortunately, signing a "Durable Power of Attorney" also carries with it the feeling of giving up one's independence, a sense of loss. This should not be the case, but should be a relief to the patient. This should be merely "planning for the future" so the patient can receive adequate care.

Along with the Power of Attorney should be instructions for using this gift of trust. In my father's situation, he wanted me to have this power; and indeed he provided for it about ten years before his death. At that time my father communicated his desires to me, the eldest daughter. It was not difficult for him. He was trying to be certain that his family was aware of his love and concern for us, and he was planning for his future. I did not feel the need to write any instructions down. My relationship with my sisters was and is such that they too had trust in my decisions. But in some situations it might be wise to write down and record your conversation with your loved one so there will be no misunderstandings among family members.

Another reason to have power of attorney is that, in the event you must take over the checkbook, the savings account, or other financial matters while the patient is still living, you are able to do so easily. You must keep in mind, however, that you are responsible for each penny you spend, and that you should keep accounts for the rest of your family and for the lawyer to see how the money has been spent. In addition, it may be difficult emotionally to use this power of attorney—it certainly was for me. Yet it provided the funds that were necessary to care for my father's financial matters when he was too ill to think about it.

The Durable Power of Attorney can be changed with a simple signature. Check the laws in your state, and talk with an attorney to be certain all is in order.

Durable Power of Attorney for Health Care, the Living Will

In some states the Durable Power of Attorney for Health Care is a provision that ensures that the patient's wishes are respected in the event the person is unable to make health care decisions. It also provides legal protection that assures that the patient's wishes will be followed. It is important to find out what is available in your state in order to be able to follow your patient's wishes. In the Durable Power of Attorney for Health Care, there are special legal protections for doctors who follow the decision made by the person who has that power.

The safeguards built into this power of attorney for health care give the responsible person the authority to make decisions only if the patient is incapable of doing so. Written instructions from the patient will generally be legally binding and valid for a set number of years. He or she may terminate this power at any time by simply telling either the doctor or the appointed person that he or she no longer wants it to be effective.[7]

The question of resuscitation, being on life support systems, and withholding care are hot topics. For the Christian, this brings up such questions as the meaning of life and the meaning of suffering. One of the biggest fears for many is being kept alive, needlessly, when death is eminent. Modern technology has changed our life expectancy so we not only are living longer, but also, in many cases, we could be sustained for a long period of time. Many deal with the situation by requesting that they not be kept alive unnecessarily by life-supporting methods. Facing suffering is a huge topic, one which such a book as this cannot deal with adequately. No one chooses to suffer, but suffering is a part of life, and no one is immune. We can identify with Christ's suffering for us in just a small way. In addition, suffering and trials bring growth and development in our lives.

Ultimately, the decision is a personal matter. There is a time to resuscitate—when life could be spared and a person could live many months, even years. But when the person is close to death, one might appear to be tampering with another life if called upon to resuscitate. It was difficult for me to face the fact that my father said, "I do not want to be resuscitated. I do not want to be on life-support. When the time comes, I am ready to die." One of my biggest fears and gnawing uncertainties as a caregiver was, "Will I know what to do when the time comes? How can I *not* call 911?" That question was answered when I needed it.

Some people say ending life or knowing when the end has come, as well as the nuances of euthanasia, will be the issue of the 1990s as abortion has been for the 1980s. The end of life certainly raises a lot of questions—ones that the dying and their caregivers will need to address in some way or another. "Many faiths—traditionally committed to defending the sanctity of human life—endorse the idea of withholding extraordinary life-prolonging measures from the terminally ill. But deep divisions exist about who has the right to terminate life—and at what point."[8]

This book cannot possibly address this issue. More or less, the caregiver and patient must struggle with the decisions to be made. They need to pray that God will make it clear when His time is right for the patient to leave this earth. "At the bedside level," says Marsha Fowler of Azusa Pacific University, who trains nurses to work as staff members of local churches, "the single most important bioethical issue . . . is the way in which one goes about dying—withholding treatment and withdrawing treatment once it's started; and how you evaluate this in terms of the person's spiritual walk and beliefs."[9]

Caregiving is indeed a difficult position in which to be. Since life and death are ultimately in God's hands, and even though the patient may at times want to die and not be a burden, God may have a purpose for the suffering. Thus we can only pray that the patient and the caregiver can trust God's sovereignty.

The caregiver needs to be there with and for the patient at all times during the caregiving. "Hospice staff will tell you that those who ask to end life no longer ask for that when they feel they are not abandoned, when they feel they are cared for, and when they have adequate pain control," says Corrine Bayley, vice president for ethics and corporate values at St. Joseph Health System in Orange, California.[10]

If you as caregiver have any questions or need to talk with someone about this issue, try speaking with your pastor.

Should the Patient Draw Up a Living Trust?

This is probably one of the most difficult decisions for a person to make. Check with a lawyer and find out what the requirements are in your state.

A Living Trust will certainly simplify the handling of the estate. In many cases it can also be a way to avoid probate and taxes after the patient is deceased. Depending on the size of the estate and the state laws, it will undoubtedly save a great deal of headache in the future. It takes some time and a fair amount of work for the caregiver, if the patient is not able to draw up the Living Trust on his or her own. But you must see that it is done. There also will be doctor and hospital bills, as well as insurance policies, to deal with following death. This one effort to draw up a

Living Trust will greatly reduce the many things to do in the future. Your life will be much simpler, and things can be cared for after death in a more expeditious manner.

I advise the patient, the caregiver, or both to obtain a lawyer to handle this for you. You will be certain that it is done correctly, and you will have guidelines to follow to ensure it is all cared for properly. If you cannot afford a lawyer, there are community services available that will guide you through the process and often volunteers help with such matters. Also seek a lawyer's advice on giving the total estate as a gift before death. It may be that the patient is ready and financially able to do this, which will certainly simplify the entire process.

Talk about Distribution of the Estate

If the patient decides on a Living Trust, he or she will probably want to draw up a will to accompany it. If the decision is against a Living Trust, a will is absolutely necessary in order to protect the estate so it will end up according to the patient's wishes.

It is a good idea to discuss with the family what has been done. If possible, the patient should talk about how the estate should be handled and even the rationale with which the assets are being divided. These assets may not be extensive, but for even the smallest estate it is wise to put things in good order. Some people are leaving a videotape of their wishes and the rationale for the decisions they make. This helps the recipients of the estate not only appreciate what has been done, but also hopefully to avoid misunderstanding among the heirs. Many families, even those who are solid and close, have been fractured following the disposition of an estate because of the way it was handled. The division of material things, which are temporal, most often causes trouble.

Even though it may be difficult to talk about a will, gifting, or a living trust, there will be a tremendous amount of relief when they are taken care of.

Plan for Visits from Family Members

Family members need and want to spend time with the patient, particularly the dying loved one, both for their own sakes and for the patient's. But it is essential that everyone not come at once, particularly if the patient is very ill, is clinging to a hope that is keeping him or her alive, or still has some time left but is too sick to have much company. It is likely that all of the family will want to come immediately. But the patient is not always ready for extensive visitation. In fact, the patient may request that family members wait to come for a visit. The onslaught of visitors can be a signal to the patient that the end is near (which it may be) and he or she may not be ready to face that reality quite yet. Or in the case of the young person, it just may be too tiring for their well-being and recuperation.

It is difficult for the caregiver to handle family and close friends. The caregiver wants to protect the patient, particularly if she or he is newly diagnosed with cancer, undergoing chemotherapy, and trying to stay strong, well, and germ-free. The caregiver can become caught between the patient and the visitor, if the patient does not want to see the visitor. The caregiver is in the unfortunate position of trying to decipher the patient's true wishes, the prognosis, the motives of the family member who desperately wants to come and visit, and the well-being of the patient. In addition, the caregiver must deal with the knowledge of the patient's life-expectancy.

Without getting into family politics and trying to give any solutions to the situation, I can only suggest that the caregiver try to space out the visits. Even at the risk of being misunderstood by the family, the caregiver should put the patient's well-being first and simply say no if it is necessary. The caregiver can devise a plan—a schedule— for the family and extended family to follow and stick to that. But be careful to have the visitors come for only a short duration. Depending on the living situation, whether the patient is in the hospital, at home, or a nursing home, the visitor should be kept to short, manageable visits. If you have set certain standards of health and cleanliness, abide strictly to them. Let the visitors know that if they have a cold or other sickness they must wear a surgical mask. If the patient is undergoing chemotherapy and has other illnesses that makes him or her susceptible to infections, the patient can wear a surgical mask. If children are involved, they should only stay for a very short amount of time. The visits must be peaceful; no unpleasant subjects are to be discussed; no family gossiping or complaining, and, most certainly, no arguments. If this happens, you must step in and protect the patient. You may feel like a jail warden or a police officer, but ultimately, you are responsible for the patient and the atmosphere.

Make the Funeral Plans

Planning for the patient's funeral, particularly with the Christian, can be a very rewarding and enjoyable experience, especially if you do it early on while the patient is still feeling relatively well. It is an affirmation of the patient's hope of heaven. Let the patient choose the music, the pastor(s), the Scripture, and the place for the service to be held.

If the patient has not already done so, you will need to plan for the casket, minister's honorarium, whether or not to have flowers or other honorariums, instructions for the burial site, how to pay for the arrangements, and the choice of headstone and inscription. If they wish cremation, those details also need to be decided. If these arrangements have not been made, they should be done right away.

It is also helpful to prepare the obituary, the death notice, ahead of time. You can gather the information from the patient, old records, and family history if need be. You will be surprised how difficult it is to remember everything at the time of death and how helpful it is to have this taken care of early. One of my sisters did this task for our family long before it was needed, and it was a tremendous relief.

One of the special memories I have during my father's stay with us was of the morning we spent planning his funeral. He dictated, and I wrote down the songs he requested. Then he chose the pastors, the Scripture, and the part he wanted each pastor to have in the services. In his case he had a funeral and burial in one city, and a memorial service in another. The services were not only ones that he had planned, but they also focused on what his life had stood for—which was to glorify God. And that showed through. It made the services special times of remembrance and honor to God to know that Daddy had a part in planning them.

Even if a funeral is not something that you would normally talk about with the patient, it still is something that you as caregiver should suggest. If other members of the family can be there where you actually plan with the patient, this can be a special time of fellowship and bonding together for all.

After the arrangements have been finished, place the information in a file (the obituary, service outline, along with instructions for the funeral home, what to do at the time of death, etc.). Keep it handy so at the time of death you can respond with action and won't have to stop and think about the details.

Telephone Numbers to Call at Death

1. Doctor (Notify doctor and ask for signature on death certificate.)
2. Home nurse or doctor (Ask for verification of death at home.)
3. Family (Have it set up so you will call one person, and that person will call the others.)
4. Funeral home (Ask them to send a hearse/ambulance.)

5. Pastor (Inform the church. You will need their support during the next few hours.)
6. Others whom you think should know immediately. (Inform neighbors, close friends, etc.)

In many cases, when the patient is elderly and has moved from another state, the burial will be in that state. If so, you need to choose a local funeral home that will work with the primary one (the out-of-state funeral home). If an autopsy is necessary, the local funeral home will need to take care of this procedure, and they will need to know immediately upon death. The local funeral home will prepare the body and then will make arrangements to ship the body by airplane or hearse, if the primary home is within driving distance. In any event you should have the details worked out so that, night or day, you only need to call the primary funeral home, who will communicate with the local facility.

One important thing to know: If you do NOT want the patient resuscitated, check your state laws. In some states you must not call 911. Paramedics in most states are required by law to resuscitate the patient if they are called to the scene. The best thing is to plan ahead with your doctor so he or she can give you exact instructions on what you should do. This may vary from state to state and from doctor to doctor. If the patient is in a nursing home, the requirements may be different. You will need to check them out with the doctor and have the appropriate documentation necessary to carry out the patient's wishes.

Plan Ahead for Keeping the Patient at Home

Many patients prefer to die at home. Caregivers often choose this as well. It can be a very rewarding experience, as has been the case in our family. But this option for caregiving means that you must look at your present living situation and make short- or long-term adjustments. The basic needs are a comfortable room close to a bathroom, doors that allow wheelchair and walker access, easy access or a wheelchair ramp to the outside, and bathroom fixtures (hold bars) by the toilet and in the shower. A light fixture that can be reached by the patient, a space heater, a comfortable chair, a bedside table, and a television, cassette player, radio, or other items are also helpful.

You may need to plan ahead and have some remodeling done or to rearrange your present living situation to some extent. Are there stairs to climb? Will you need to provide for some kind of a "lift"? And so on.

Be certain that you have a place where the patient can look out a window, and if possible a bright, cheery atmosphere. A coat of paint or a colored comforter, pillow, and throws can make a room look more pleasant.

Visit a Prospective Nursing Home

While the older, terminally ill patient is still somewhat ambulatory, it is important to investigate the option of a full-care facility in the event that one becomes necessary. If the patient is willing and open, it will help him or her to at least drive by the facility or see some brochures. This will begin to prepare the patient for the eventuality that care in such a facility may be necessary, should life be prolonged and the circumstances warrant it. Knowing that this is available may give a sense of relief to you, the caregiver, as well as to the patient.

Is planning ahead overwhelming? It certainly may seem so, but if you take just one thing at a time, one day at a time, the accomplishment of preparing for the future will give you the peace of mind that all is in order. And may the God of order give you clarity of mind as you tackle the load.

CHAPTER FIVE
Some Practical Helps for Caregiving

Let's pretend that you, the caregiver, become the patient. Put yourself in that situation: You are confined to bed and are chair-bound or wheelchair-bound most of the time. You can walk some, but you don't have the energy. You want to get up and be with the family, but you don't have the physical resources. Your mind says "you can do it," but your body won't cooperate. You feel frustrated and discouraged.

Because you want to go for a short walk, you build up your courage. But the steps you take are too painful and debilitating to the rest of your body. You begin to feel woozy.

You want to talk with your visitor, but your attention is waning. You appreciate her coming, but the one hour visit has drained your efforts to even talk. You want to sleep.

The pain is just beginning but you say to yourself, "I don't need much medication. I am feeling great." You stand up to head toward the bathroom, and you shift your body. The pain is excruciating! It's like nothing you can describe to another person. So you sit back down, ask for more medication and for assistance to walk, and possibly you even admit that you need to be pushed to the bathroom in the wheelchair.

A patient who is virtually chair-bound or bed-bound has a very limited world, which has physically trapped him or her in a small, sometimes mundane and lifeless location. The patient's world consists of you (the caregiver), other members of the family and friends who still come for visits, the television, radio, CD or cassette player, and maybe a view out of a window.

There are many variations on the above scenario. Some are better, and some are much, much worse.

The caregiver probably does not have the time to sit and think about the patient's world. And yet I feel that is one of the most important and practical concerns for the well-being of the patient. I also wish that hospitals would realize that the psychological environment for the patient should be positive, pleasant, have some kind of view out of a window (the hospital beds always seem to be facing away from the window), and that the atmosphere should be as happy and upbeat as is possible — even up to death.

Many of the following suggestions are written for the caregiver who is caring for the older patient at home. Most of them can be adapted to the younger person or the elderly in a nursing home, care facility, or hospice.

Reminisce with the Elderly Patient

The dignity and worth of the older person is vital to understanding and empathizing with them. Many older people, particularly when they are facing the inevitability of death, can be depressed and withdrawn, and they can feel very insignificant. Elizabeth Brown says, "One of the most important things in dealing with the elderly is to make a commitment to reminisce with the patient. The oral history, the journaling of one's life, is so important. The older person is in decline, things have changed, and there is an increase in confusion.

"The pattern of life has been interrupted, and this causes tremendous feelings of loss of worth and dignity. In some cases they have been placed in an inmate mentality.

We have socialized them into a dependent mode and made them totally dependent. In situations where the elderly are confused and in decline, often unable to cope with their situation, remarkable changes have taken place in their outlook toward life when they have been a part of a 'reminiscing group.' "

This can be done anywhere, at home with a caregiver, in a hospital room, or in a nursing home. Recall the hymns and play a tape of some of the music that the patient knew and loved in years past. Music therapy is a wonderful way to bring joy to the patient. There is often a significant change and decrease in confusion when the patient talks about the smells, tastes, sounds, and experiences from his or her past.

Ask questions like "What was the first thing you noticed as you came in the door when you came home from school?" This reinforcement and reassurance of background and experience can give the older person a sense of dignity and worth. Someone cares enough to talk about his or her life. It is amazing the changes that occur when an elderly patient takes part in remembering his or her past. Even in the worst of situations, reminiscing gives perspective to the current-day trauma he or she is experiencing. It doesn't take much time to talk for a few minutes with a patient, even each week. In addition, a brief amount of time focused on the patient and his or her past can give handles for the patient to grab onto and a sense of security.

Caring for the Physically Disabled or an Ill Young Person

The focus of this book is primarily on caregiving for the elderly, but many of the areas addressed can be adapted for the younger person who is physically disabled, has suffered a tragic accident, or may be chronically or terminally ill. Robert Vander Zaag, whose young daughter contracted polio, reflected on his experiences and gives the following advice to those who may be caring for a child or young adult in a similar situation.

1. Treat the child as normally as possible from the very beginning. Don't allow the "world owes me a living" syndrome to develop.

2. Assign chores around the house within the limits of the child's capabilities.

3. Develop the child's self-esteem. The child must be made aware of the fact that he or she has qualities that are admirable by anyone's definition.

4. Instill in the child a "go for it" attitude. The child must be made to understand that *handicapped* does not mean *helpless*. As William James said, "Anything the mind can conceive and believe, it can achieve."

5. Encourage constantly. It takes more courage for the physically disabled than for others to face life and its trials.

6. When the physically disabled child gets down about his or her condition, the child doesn't necessarily need a pep talk. The child might need someone with whom to empathize and cry for a few minutes until he or she can regroup. This is not difficult since the parent may feel like crying more often than the child.

7. Always be there to help the child maintain a good perspective. Actually everyone has some kind of a handicap. There are many people with far worse handicaps than the physically disabled.

8. It is important for the young person to know how very proud their parents are of him or her. The child needs to hear about it often, especially when about to lose perspective and focus on the handicap rather than on strengths and capabilities.

9. Physical contact is crucial. Sitting beside the child and holding him or her is often far more important than anything you can say. Realize that a child's nightmare is that you might be taken away, and realize that your holding the child is a wonderful boost to that all-important sense of security. The world is a safe place when Mom or Dad enfolds the child with loving and capable arms.

These guidelines are helpful not only for the disabled, but also for the child or young person who may have gone through some other traumatic illness and need long-term care while recuperating.

Environment

Take a look at the setting where your patient spends the majority of time. Is the patient's furniture situated to give the best view, hopefully out a window? Is there a tree or a street outside where there is activity to observe? Where does the sunshine hit, and at what hours of the day? Is the room light? If the room is dark, is it possible to have a coat of paint applied? Does the room have a plant in it? Are there too many plants so that the patient feels suffocated? Sit in the patient's chair and observe. Lie in the patient's bed and see the view. Would you want to spend your last days in this environment? This applies to the home, the nursing home, and a hospital room.

Here are some inexpensive suggestions for making the environment cozy and comfortable. First of all, choose colors that the patient likes, but remember that the darker colors are more depressing and that pastels seem to calm.

Does your environment include a flower or two? After a few weeks, the flowers will stop coming for the patient because the hospital visits will become more ordinary. Once a person has given flowers, it is unusual for that person to bring more. Cut flowers from the yard—a single rose now and then. Or bring a grocery-store bouquet once in a while. It will always seem to cheer the patient. A silk flower, which you can replace frequently, adds a bit of color and cheer to a room. Even if the patient seems too weak to appreciate the environment, it is still the environment. And possibly you and those who care for the patient need that boost as well.

A bird feeder outside the window (we have humming-birds in our area) can bring hours of enjoyment and pre-occupation for the patient. Keep a pair of binoculars at the bedside so the patient can enjoy the birds, squirrels, and other outdoor life up close. This activity can bring great enjoyment, even when the patient is totally bedridden and in great pain or discomfort. A fishbowl or tank in the patient's room, if it is convenient, also brings enjoyment and diversion.

The patient should have a few of his or her knickknacks and pictures that are especially important and that bring nostalgia. My father had photos of his special friends, children, grandchildren, and his wife. He enjoyed just looking at the pictures, praying, and loving them. We also had several pictures that were hung on his walls—one was a painting of his Florida home and lake that he dearly loved and missed (painted for him by one of his granddaughters). One idea that seems to be helpful and keeps things from being mundane is to change the picture(s) on the wall frequently. Even a colorful poster or a wall hanging with an interesting pattern can give new energy and enjoyment to the patient. If it is appropriate, a bulletin board can be used for this purpose. Greeting cards can be posted there for a few days at a time, and then rotated. My father enjoyed some of the children's art that was sent by young friends.

The patient's environment probably will not change on its own. Therefore, you, the caregiver, must be the one to change it for the patient to avoid monotony and bring new life and interest in simple, subtle ways. This may be one thing that another member of the family can do to help, assuming that the person understands the need and can provide things that would be appropriate. Just remember that too much change may be difficult for the patient to handle. The personal items, photos, knickknacks, and special treasures should be left intact as the patient desires.

The caregiver must try to wear attractive colors and look well kept. This is important since you are the one person whom the patient sees day in and day out. This is also probably one of the hardest things to do, but it really is helpful to avoid blacks, grays, and other dark colors unless you dress them up with colorful sweaters, blouses, or jackets. You'll feel better about yourself as well.

It is important to keep the clutter level to a minimum. This may become difficult since the patient's room and environment are often quite small and cramped. Some things are important to have around, others seem to stay in piles, because the desire of the patient is to have them—although there is not sufficient energy to read, look at, write, or respond to these books, pamphlets, papers, and letters. A basket in which to keep miscellaneous clutter will at least keep things neat and will give the patient the sense that you are not throwing things out but keeping them together in place for possible future use.

Color, light, a window with a view, flowers, pictures, and enough change in the patient's world to avoid monotony and bring joy are important elements of the environment that need to be considered and cared for. Life for you and the patient will be more peaceful and joyful.

Correspondence

Correspondence is critical to the feelings of self-worth by the patient. This cannot be stressed enough. If I have learned anything from caregiving, it is how important it is to keep in touch, even with just a short note or card. And this is not an easy thing to do when one is not naturally inclined to write letters. But, I repeat, it is most important.

At first the patient will receive many cards and letters from friends who are experiencing the shock at the news of his or her illness. This will taper off within a short amount of time, particularly if it is necessary for the patient to relocate to another part of the country. There will be the faithful friends who support, love, and call the patient, even up until the very end. Some people, however, just can't handle that kind of ongoing support. This is often difficult for the patient to understand. There is almost a feeling of abandonment, loss, and being set aside by those with whom they had once been connected. The caregiver needs to help the patient understand why and how people react to terminal, chronic, or long-term illnesses. It is also important to try to keep up with those friends and family who continue to be supportive and caring, even from a distance.

A way to do this is to buy a number of greeting cards or postcards for the patient to send. You, the caregiver, may need to address them for the patient. And then you may need to write them—dictated by the patient. These cards help keep the patient connected with loved ones and friends, and they also show love and support. Many times, the patient will want to pray regularly for those friends.

Telephone Calls

The telephone is a lifeline to other family members, friends, and the occasional business that needs to be dealt with by the patient. But, as is true in all of life, there are times when there is a lull in receiving these calls. People get busy in the natural course of life. They don't forget to call, but they put it off until there is a convenient time.

One practical suggestion for you as the caregiver: Devise a plan for your family by which you can give them a brief call and ask them to call the patient. This became one way that my sisters knew our father was feeling a bit down, and it included them in the caregiving as well. They were able to be a part of his life when he needed them, and I could share the responsibility with them from a distance. I also did this at the very end of Daddy's life with his brothers and sister, knowing that the time was short and that he would want to visit with them, and they with him one last time. It helped him tie up loose ends, in a sense, and he died having talked with them, and they knowing they were loved and thought about up until the end.

Be sure the calls are not too long. There may be times when the patient can handle only a brief "I love you" call.

Ways to Include the Family in the Patient's Life

We've already talked about telephone calls, cards, and letters, and some original art provided by family members.

There are some other practical ways to allow those close to the patient to be involved in the special care. Suggest that these people use their gifts of art, music, poetry, handiwork, and so forth to provide enjoyment.

The patient can enjoy an album of pictures on a particular subject many times during the illness. One granddaughter made a needlepoint Scripture verse and put it in the plastic cover of a picture album. Another collected favorite pictures of the family and put them inside the album. A close friend did a cross-stitch of a favorite Scripture verse, and put it on a candy jar that was placed in the patient's room. Another grandchild wrote special letters to his grandfather. An album can contain letters and cards from friends—assurances that those people are remembering the patient and are praying.

Some other ideas are taping music of singing or playing an instrument on video or audio cassette. Send, or have sent, video tapes of special school events such as band or other musical performances, sermons and church services, or other special events. Telling stories and jokes provides a much-needed lift to the spirits. Visiting by videotape or cassette is becoming more and more a viable option these days. And the possibilities of using a fax machine for instant communication with loved ones is just beginning. Let your imagination go. Be creative and explore new ways of caring. And include friends and family from a distance.

Music plays an important role for many older people, as in this case: "Mother couldn't talk, because she had had a stroke," says Doris Stephens whose mother was in a nursing home for several years. "But sometimes she recognized me. The funny thing was that even though she couldn't say anything, she could hum the tunes of the hymns that she had known."

Diversions for the Patient

Of course, the amount of energy that the patient can use varies from day to day. A lot depends on the patient's mental and physical condition and other variables, such as location (rural, urban, etc.). But hopefully these ideas will help you think creatively and will encourage you to seek ways to keep the patient living a somewhat palliative life.

Former caregiver Marjorie Stiles, a registered nurse, says, "I have learned that it is important to do special things, as long as the patient is able to do so, such as going out for a hamburger, or going to a special place for lunch, one that the patient has enjoyed in the past. These mean so much to the patient, just to get out of the house, even if there is not always the remembrance of these things."

Community Involvement

There are opportunities in some communities for the patient to become involved. For instance, one can tutor children or adults in a particular subject (English as a Second Language, specific subjects such as history, or some other area of knowledge and experience). During my father's illness, we had a young Hispanic woman clean house once a week. My father enjoyed speaking Spanish with her—and she enjoyed him. He could not have spent big blocks of time visiting with her, but a few minutes of time was quite a nice diversion for him.

Cassette Tapes

Books on tape can bring hours of enjoyment. Language tapes hold interest for some patients. Tapes of church services, particularly from one's home church, are very welcomed by older people, as are tapes of the spoken Bible.

The Public Library

The library is a good source of videos and can include travel, classic movies, and special interests (my father's favorites were those on boating and fishing, two of his most enjoyable hobbies). Younger people will enjoy cartoons, old classics, and upbeat movies on video.

Many more titles are being added as the market expands, and these can be checked out for free in most places. Large picture books for the elderly are also available on many subjects, as are large posters and prints of famous paintings. Keep abreast of these resources. We made the library a regular stop on our outings. Although my father did not have the strength or energy to spend much time looking, he did enjoy walking in and out and seeing the people. In fact, I had to go by myself at another time to discover just what was available and report back to him. Thus he was able to make a choice from my selection list. I sometimes chose two or three at a time since the subject matter to be enjoyed might depend on how my father was feeling and what he was interested in watching on a particular evening.

Crossword Puzzles and Other Activities

These can be a good diversion for those who are still able to think and ponder. There comes a point, however, when that takes too much energy, and unless the patient is doing it with someone else, it becomes a chore. But simple crossword puzzles should still be available for such a time as they can be enjoyed.

For children and young people, a new activity or a gift to unwrap each week is something to look forward to for the child. It need not be expensive. A book, toy, hair ribbon, puzzle, or tape can bring enjoyment. You, another family member, or friend should buy several such gifts to be given regularly or at a particularly discouraging time to add fun and joy to the patient's life. It is also important for the child or young person to have gifts to give to other children that are in similar situations. It gives the patient an opportunity to care for others as well.

Relaxation Tape

A relaxation tape of hymns, Christian music, and/or classical music is a lifesaver. It is important to use music that the patient enjoys and feels comfortable with. This is not the time to help the patient learn and appreciate new music. And it probably is not the time to have music that has a strong, heavy beat and is more excitable. You, the caregiver, must be the judge of the patient's needs. And this will be a time when you may have to listen to the kind of music that you personally would not choose. Music soothes — and music is a gift from God. Music can be tremendously helpful and encouraging to the patient, even though he or she may not be able to express it. And music on tape or radio is a comfort and gives a sense of being connected, particularly during the nighttime hours when the patient is alone and cannot sleep.

During the last few days of my father's life, he enjoyed old hymns and Gospel songs. We had saved a tape of piano music for such a time and, as he died, the music was playing.

A Shortwave Radio

This is a hobby of many older people and it can be an interesting diversion, giving incentive to hear what is going on around the world. It's always challenging and fun to find some new station far away.

Food

The way you prepare and present food will sometimes help entice the patient to eat a bit more. Patterned or colored napkins purchased during a grocery store trip can add interest to the table or tray. For children, special cartoon or animal characters on napkins or place mats are fun. Have someone from the extended family keep on the lookout for interesting napkins, and send them to you. Using different colored or patterned dishes interchangeably is also a way to keep the look of the food interesting. Our daughter found a fascinating mug with a lid for her grandfather. He enjoyed using it because of the giver. And the lid was a practical way to keep his coffee or tea warm if he didn't feel like drinking it right away.

Colored straws for shakes, juices, and other drinks add some freshness. And we often served afternoon tea in china cups. Remember when your children enjoyed tea parties? This is the same idea! Not a lot of food is eaten, but every little bit helps keep up the spirit and adds a bit of joy for the patient—and the caregiver!

Stickers and Candles

There are many stickers available in patterns, animals, colors, stars, other shapes, and even some words. You can purchase these stickers for a minimal amount of money at gift and greeting card stores. You can use them as decorative cards for the tray or table, or for cards to be put beside the bed or chair. Young and old alike enjoy these stickers.

Candles are a must for the evening meals. The more attractive the setting, the more likely the patient will enjoy eating even those few mandatory bites of food. And the more the caregiver will enjoy these brief times with the patient.

Trips and Outings

Elsewhere in this book we discussed the importance of trips and outings for both the patient and the caregiver. It may not be possible to find a spot where you can sit by water—an ocean, lake, or river. But a park with trees, a spot in an urban setting where there are people to watch, or a ride down a street where the houses or environment are interesting can be a very good outing. In some situations the caregiver may not drive. Thus if it is at all possible, the caregiver should either hire a friend or a taxi, or find some way to have an occasional outing, even if it is just a wheelchair ride around the neighborhood.

Clothes

Clothes are seemingly unimportant to the patient. But clothes do continue to portray the image of who the person is to the caregiver, friends, and family who visit occasionally, doctors who see the patient in their offices, and the rest of the world with whom the patient is in contact. Even though the patient may not feel like dressing, you should encourage cleanliness, neatness, and good personal hygiene. The patient will most likely be appreciative of your efforts.

A new, colorful sweater, blouse, or shirt will boost spirits. When the body shape changes with the illness, it may be necessary to buy new clothes for the patient. Even though this may seem like a wasted expense, it will bring a great deal of dignity to the patient to be able to wear comfortable and well-fitting clothes. It will be difficult for the caregiver to do this kind of shopping. When a special item of clothing is needed, it is impossible for the caregiver to go from store to store, or even to call many stores. This is when a friend or family member who lives out of town can help out. Catalog shopping is also a convenient way to take care of this need. Most stores have 800 numbers and can rush items to you. Local department stores can also be convenient and easy to use.

A new nightgown or pair of pajamas is a boost for the home-and-bed-bound patient. It's amazing to see how eyes light up at such a gift. The simple pleasures of life become so important for young and old alike.

Magazine Subscriptions

Magazines provide continued contact with the world and bring mail to the patient, even though he or she may not be able to read a lot. The pictures and captions can communicate, and a magazine format provides for short snippets of reading time. Subscribe to a special magazine, such as *Fisherman's World, House and Garden,* National Geographic's *World* for children, and Focus on the Family's *Clubhouse, Clubhouse Junior, Brio,* and *Breakaway* children and youth magazines. Or subscribe to a magazine that is from a favorite city, such as Dallas, Atlanta, and Los Angeles, etc. A few dollars are worth the enjoyment.

Furniture and Other Items

Furniture for the patient is very important. There are new businesses that are thriving in the home care areas, providing everything from hospital beds, oxygen, walkers, bedside hospital tables to commodes that are placed over the toilet for the patient who cannot sit and stand up easily. There are hookups available for feeding tube bags and other medications, and the options are growing as the field quickly advances. It was comforting for us to know that all of these things were available, that the bedroom could become a hospital room so the patient could be cared for at home as long as possible.

Your household furniture may not be comfortable for the patient. In our case we needed to purchase several recliners, since that was the only kind of chair my father could sit on with relative comfort. Be sure to try out the furniture before you purchase it. We found that a recliner that turns around was very convenient. The patient can be a part of the world at 360 degrees and can remain active in turning the chair on his or her own to some extent.

Suggestion: purchase the chair(s) or other furniture early in the patient's illness, so the patient can be a part of the shopping and choice. Then it will be the patient's chair—a comfort to have his or her very own furniture in the caregiver's home. Often furniture stores have a thirty-day return or exchange policy. Ask before you purchase because the patient may not like what you buy.

At the writing of this book, I have just returned from a week of caring for my 102-year-old grandmother who has spent three months recuperating from a fall in which she damaged her frail backbone. She has been chair-bound, unable to stand and sit on her own. We purchased an electric lift chair and outfitted her walker with wheels in the front. Within minutes she was able to stand, sit, and walk on her own. A physical therapist has fitted her with a back brace for additional support and my grandmother has a new "lease on life," a change in attitude, a break out of her depression, and a freedom to get around in her own home again without the need for twenty-four-hour assistance.

Another item of furniture that we put to good use with

my father was our tea cart, designed with three trays, which could be rolled from room to room. This was set up as a permanent side table. On it were placed items that my father might want: Bible, books and magazines, correspondence, greeting cards, photo album, radio/cassette player with clock, intercom unit, and a tray for drinks, food, and medications. This became his table.

Bathroom fixtures for the disabled can be purchased at a discount home supply store. Flannel sheets and pillow cases are a God-send for helping the patient keep warm and comfortable, whereas cotton or percale is oftentimes cold for the patient. Egg-crate foam mattresses that are available at the hospital or department store are well worth the expense and give much comfort to the patient. I always insisted that one be put on my father's bed, even if he were in the hospital for only a one-day treatment. The pain and discomfort that can be experienced from not having it is not worth it.

Intercom Unit and Other Devices

An inexpensive intercom unit can be a lifesaver for the caregiver, particularly if the house is so large that you're away from the patient for any length of time. If the patient needs assistance to get up and down out of bed or the chair, or if there is a problem, the patient need only push the button, and you are instantly aware that you are wanted. The units can be purchased at a discount home-supply company, and they are well worth the investment. We purchased three and carried one of them with us from room to room, while one was with my father on his table and the other was kept by his bedside. I think he enjoyed the fact that he was in close touch with the family, even while we may have been in another part of the house.

A television set with headphones and remote control is helpful for the patient to have, either in the room at home where the patient spends the most time or in the patient's nursing home room. A VCR also brings much enjoyment. During my father's time with us, we subscribed to the

Disney Channel, a nice diversion. A cable station hookup might be helpful for the nursing home patient as well.

Handicapped Sticker

Even though your patient may not be psychologically ready, obtain a handicapped sticker for your car early in the caregiving. If you put it off, it is just one more thing you must do later, and it is more difficult to obtain when the patient really needs it. Psychologically the patient is facing so many things at that point that it is just one more downer. A handicapped sticker means a lot when you are going for outings in parks or other settings, as well as for doctors' office visits. The sticker is available for a small fee at your Department of Motor Vehicles, but you will need a doctor's prescription in order to obtain it. Be certain that the doctor prescribes plenty of months ahead. When the doctor put a three-month limit on one for my father, Daddy said, "I guess he's not expecting me to live long." Indeed, he lived almost a year longer than anticipated.

Health Precautions

When you begin your caregiving activities, one of the first things to do is to purchase a good antiseptic cleaner, rubber gloves, and even surgical masks. The environment should be as clean and sanitized as possible. This is not only important for the patient, but also for the caregiver. It is critical that each person handling food, washing dishes, cleaning, and cooking be extra careful to keep hands washed and away from one's face. We used surgical masks in preparing food and sterilizing dishes during my father's chemotherapy. And we used the masks during times when we had colds or allergy infections. This is absolutely critical for staying healthy and well for both caregiver and patient.

Visits to the dentist, the optometrist, and other medical professionals should not be overlooked, even though the patient may be dying. Again, the dignity and well-being of the patient is foremost up to the end. In fact, our optome-

trist visited my father to adjust his glasses the day before
he died. Of course, we did not know the end was near,
but we did know it wouldn't be long. My father's glasses,
however, were so uncomfortable on his nose that they
needed adjusting. (That one-time visit remarkably affected
our optometrist. He still talks about it two years later.)
These small, but again, very important parts of the patient's well-being are integral to a quality of life that is
needed for one's personal self-worth and dignity. Don't
give up on them. And do try to arrange for home visits if
the patient is completely bedridden. Many professionals
would be happy to accommodate your request.

Visitors

Encourage and arrange for visitors, but set limits. Again,
from my experience my father had certain wishes in this
area, and there were certain people that he did not want
to have with him for any length of time. This was particularly true of children. As much as he loved them, their
activity bothered him. And some adults did not know
when to just be with him or when to talk. Depending on
his pain tolerance, he could not manage long visits. I realized I had to take control of the situation and be a buffer
for him, and I did so, even though I risked being misunderstood. One caution I can give other caregivers: When a
visitor comes, begin by stating the fact that the patient can
have visitors only for a few minutes, and then the patient
will be too worn out. You as caregiver can sometimes
perceive whether the visit is too long, and you can help
the visitor understand that time is over. It's a Catch–22.
The patient needs and wants visitors, but cannot endure a
visit without becoming too tired. The time of day of the
visit may make a difference too.

When hospital visitors come, be certain that they are
sensitive and do not stay for more than ten or fifteen
minutes. Again, you will probably be able to determine
what the patient can tolerate, and you must in some way
gently help the visitor to leave. One pastor visited a hospi-

tal room along with his teenaged daughter. He not only stayed for over half an hour, but also his daughter had a very bad cold. Both things were potentially detrimental to the patient's well-being.

Visits from pastors, church members, and hospital chaplains are important. It is encouraging to have someone else come to visit, pray with the patient, and administer communion in the home or hospital. This connection with the local church is vital to the sense of continuing to belong to the body of Christ.

Some Practical Medical Helps

It is not the intent of this book to address the medical aspects, other than to suggest some very practical ideas that might be helpful. It is always necessary to check medical ideas with your doctors, nurses, and other healthcare professionals. But the following suggestions are included as things that have worked in many situations:

Call the doctor when the patient's blood pressure is abnormally low and the pulse is more rapid than normal. Your doctor or nurse will give you the parameters.

It is important to monitor the bowel habits of the patient. For those who are on narcotic drugs, it is often the case that their bowels become bound up and impacted. Sometimes they need to be hospitalized for this problem. The doctor will often suggest stool softeners, or warm drinks, such as tea, coffee, hot water, prune juice, or other natural solutions, or he may prescribe a drug. One highly recommended remedy for keeping the bowel movement normal is the following:

FRUIT PASTE

Boil together for 5 minutes:
1 pound pitted prunes
1 pound raisins
1 pound figs

4 ounces of tea (boil in two-and-one-half cups of water)
Add: 1 cup brown sugar
     1 cup lemon juice
Cook together. Cool. Put mixture in food processor and blend together. Store in refrigerator. A few spoonfuls of this daily brings remarkable results, and the taste is very good.

Check the geriatric patient's skin. This is particularly necessary for the more immobile patient. If there is less protein intake, the skin of the older person will rub against the bone, causing red areas over the bony prominences. When positioning the patient, turn him or her often—every one-and-a-half to two hours to avoid skin breakdown. You can check the skin when bathing the patient. If the condition continues, one suggestion is to rub Crisco lard on the area. It stimulates the circulation and softens the skin. And of course, you will need to turn the patient more often. Frequent changing of bed linens is a must.

Suggestions for Encouraging Eating

Eating habits are often very difficult to handle for the patient and, therefore, the caregiver. Diets change frequently as the body changes and as the medication and illness affect the body. It is important to know that as people age, they lose the taste sensation for salt, but sweet things taste better—ice cream, puddings, and hard candy. The aging also find a decrease in thirst and, therefore, drink less. Yet they should be encouraged to drink a lot of liquids, and also to drink and eat calories.

For most patients, weight gain or maintenance is the goal of eating. Nutritionists and doctors offer several suggestions: (1) Increase caloric intake by eating small meals frequently. (2) At meals drink fruit juices or milkshakes instead of coffee, tea, or diet soda, since the latter create a feeling of being full and have low caloric value. (3) Boost calorie intake with milkshakes between meals. (4) Add additional calories to your meals by increasing the use of fats (particularly those unsaturated). (5) Eat dried fruits and juices; they add calories. (6) Add granola and fruit to yogurt.

For many who need extra protein, food supplements such as Ensure are prescribed by doctors for use between meals. Carnation Instant Breakfast drinks include the same ingredients, and they are less expensive. We found that adding malt, protein, a banana, other fruit, or ice cream not only added nutrition, but also tasted good.

To boost the patient's nutrition, add a teaspoon of butter or margarine to vegetables, rice, cooked cereals, and other appropriate dishes. Add yogurt or sour cream to recipes. Add raisins, nuts, and other dried fruits. Use honey in coffee or tea.

Add powdered milk to regular milk, soups, desserts, and casseroles, as it lends itself to the recipe. I added a small amount of protein powder to recipes, such as meatloaf and beef or vegetable soups. Mix peanut butter with sauces and chocolate sauce with ice cream. Add cheese to vegetables, sauces, soups, casseroles, and salads. Add ground meat to soups and casseroles.

If patients are experiencing nausea, have them eat salty foods, and stay away from sweet or greasy foods. They should drink cool, clear beverages, soups, flavored gelatin, and carbonated beverages. For diarrhea, increase fluid intake between meals, drinking juices such as peach, apricot, and pear. They should drink broth, but only a small amount at mealtime. They should eat high potassium foods such as oranges and bananas, and eat frequent meals low in roughage. And they should avoid gas-forming, spicy food.

For heartburn use mildly flavored foods and avoid greasy, fried, or spicy food. The patient should not lie down for two to three hours after eating.

For constipation regular exercise every day and a high fiber diet (whole grains, nuts, dried fruits, prune juice, and psyllium seed—Metamucil) will help the patient, who needs to drink more fluids (eight or more glasses each day). Milk of Magnesia or Senokot are effective nonprescription laxatives, but you should check with the doctor before using a laxative or stool softener.

Often the patient experiences a dry or sore mouth during radiation or chemotherapy, and thus a loss of taste. Try a soft diet of scrambled or poached eggs, puddings, and mashed potatoes. Avoid acidy, raw, or spicy foods. The patient should eat dry foods with a liquid and use cream sauces, gravies, and butter or margarine on vegetables and meat dishes.[1] Also recommended are pineapple, sugarless candy, and ice chips. Avoid commercial mouthwashes with alcohol or salt, but instead try 1 tablespoon of baking soda with one cup of warm water. If the situation is severe, ask your doctor for artificial saliva, which helps in some cases.

High Calorie Recipes

High Calorie, High Protein Milk:
Pour one quart of milk into a large bowl. Add one cup of dry skim milk and beat until dissolved. Refrigerate. (190 calories per cup.)

Juice Shake:
Three-fourths cup of fruit juice, one envelope vanilla-flavored instant breakfast, and 1½ cups of vanilla ice cream. Combine all ingredients in a blender and mix well.

Fresh Fruit Shake:
Two pieces of fresh fruit (especially banana), one-and-one-half cups of vanilla ice cream, one-third cup of milk, and three ice cubes. Combine in blender and mix well.

Basic Milkshake:
One-half cup of high calorie, high protein milk, one-half cup of cream or Mocha Mix, and one-half cup of ice cream or Mocha Mix ice cream. Beat together. (475 calories)

Milkshake variation (629 calories): Add two tablespoons of chocolate syrup or flavored powder to basic milkshake.

Buttermilk Shake (not as sweet):
One-half cup of buttermilk, one-half cup of lemonade, one-and-one-half cup of vanilla ice cream or Mocha Mix ice cream, and one envelope of eggnog-flavored instant breakfast. Blend well. (685 calories)

Puddings:
One package of instant pudding mix. Following instructions on the box, substitute high calorie/high protein milk for regular milk, or use half milk and half cream.

For patients experiencing difficulty in swallowing, regular or junior-sized jars of baby food can be used, mixed with other foods or warmed and eaten with the regular meal. These foods can be a lifesaver. Taste the food before giving it to the patient to see whether it is appealing and tasty. Mild spices, sauces, or gravies can be added to the meats, and the fruit can be served with sherbet or ice cream.

Of course there are many other kinds of diets such as low-cholesterol, lactose free, low triglyceride, salt-free, and diabetic. But all of them require special menus. The above suggestions can be adapted to the patient's particular needs. It is always a good idea to consult a dietician or nutritionist at your local hospital or community center for additional helps in adjusting the patient's diet.

As in all of caregiving, communicate with the health care professionals and use good common sense. Through trial and error, solutions will be found to meet the practical, everyday concerns for patients of all ages.

CHAPTER 6
Family, Friends, Church, and Other Support Resources

The caregiver and patient have just arrived home from the hospital. For the next few days there is a flurry of telephone calls; cards come in the mail; and people are very upset at the news of the sudden accident, life-threatening illness, terminal disease, or impending death. They all want to be there for you both. And they really mean it.

Then the reality of life settles in, and the cards and calls slow down. There comes a sense of abandonment—people have forgotten us already. Does anyone really care? This scenario can happen to anyone, no matter how many friends one has or how loved and cared for the patient may be. It's an interesting phenomena, and its effects on the patient and caregiver are substantial. Is there any way to avoid these feelings? How can both the patient and the caregiver find the support they need within a natural setting, one where both feel comfortable and secure, understood and loved?

At no other time in one's life is the need for a support system more crucial than during caregiving. And that, according to so many people, is the time when you are least likely to have the support that you need. With the initial onset of a caregiving situation, people are interested and, in fact, often very supportive. They call or send a card.

They promise to pray and be there to help you. But as a few days or weeks pass, they have gone on with their lives. The caregiver can't keep up the contact, because your life is totally wrapped up in the matters at hand—doctors' appointments, hospital visits, laundry, cooking, shopping, and giving care. You lose touch very quickly, because you become housebound and unable to keep up the friendships.

In most cases, only a few faithful and committed friends and family members will give any kind of assistance or help. Often it is surprising to see who continues to be there for you. And it is equally surprising to see who isn't. During my father's illness, some of the people whom I considered to be his close friends and my close friends never once acknowledged his illness or sent a word of encouragement and prayer support. It is hard to understand why people react the way they do to certain situations. I hurt for my father's sake, and let his hurt affect my own feelings of being slighted. But it is counterproductive to dwell on it, since there is neither rhyme nor reason to some people's reactions to other people's stress and difficulty.

One strong word of advice is appropriate here. If you are experiencing any of the above feelings of hurt or anger, don't harbor them. Pray that your attitude toward others, toward their seeming indifference to you, will be one of love in return. It's hard—but it's biblical! And most important is that you won't let your attitude affect the patient, your number-one priority. In fact, call a few friends and tell them that your loved one needs some special attention via a telephone call or card. I did this with my sisters, and (as I have stated earlier) they responded well. Their calls really buoyed up Daddy. I'm sure other friends and relatives would have been willing to contact him if they realized he needed them. As their pastor, he had stood alongside many people in their time of need. Now they could reciprocate and would have with very positive results.

Gerontologist Alana Peters says, "Many people in need of care are from dysfunctional families. We have raised a generation of children, the 'me generation,' that don't know how to take care of others. They are narcissistic and have never thought about other people." In addition to this problem, many people end up far away from loved ones and have no one to care for them.

In this time of seeming aloneness that you may feel, the caregiver and the patient both need to search out support. Where and how do you find what you need, physically, psychologically, emotionally, and spiritually? In this chapter we will address some of the needs and look for creative solutions to fill them. All caregivers must have support and encouragement, and so must the patient whose physical life is ebbing.

Family Support

Family is the God-ordained support for living and dying. God blessed us with family to love, care, and support in all ways. Our modern society has twisted the true function of family so alternate family situations exist. Divorce, remarriage, blended families, and demographics have altered the old-fashioned pattern of being born, growing, living, and dying, all usually near parents and grandparents. At one time the younger generation respected the older generation and interacted with their elders, even when they were bedridden or decrepit. Extended family members (aunts, uncles, cousins, grandchildren) were important, and family commitment to care of the elders was a given. Close friends were considered family too; and they shared a lot of life with one another.

Today, and for the future, isolation from family and longtime friends has become the norm. People are living longer, are more independent, often live far from their families and manage on their own longer. In addition, families have become fractured and distant because of many of society's problems, such as drugs, difficult divorces, misunderstandings between lifestyles and choices, generation gaps, and geographic separation.

In spite of all this turmoil, however, the family is still very important to the person who is facing a long-term illness or impending death. And the caregiver desperately needs the support of all the family. But in many situations, such as those suggested above, the primary caregiver must be a diplomat, a judge, a disciplinarian, and a secretary; and in many cases the family members will grossly misunderstand the caregiver. Nevertheless, the caregiver must keep the single focus in mind—the best interest of the patient by carrying out the patient's desires. Even in Christian families it is sometimes hard to walk the tightrope by pleasing everyone.

Communication is key to including the family in caregiving. The immediate family members need to be a part of the discussions regarding decision-making. That's your responsibility as primary caregiver. You set the tone for the caregiving setting. Even though you may not want to do it, in most family situations the primary caregiver will need to give the leadership, being certain that all who should be are included in the total decision-making process. Later on you'll be glad that you have the support from your immediate and extended family.

Communication with my sisters and other family members was very important to me. I shared the responsibility and found my family to be supportive of my decision-making. "It was important to tell Carol that she had freedom to make the decisions," said my sister Patricia Hale. "With several members of the family, two would talk, and others were left out of particular discussions. So we decided it was important to give Carol the freedom to make the decision, knowing she would do the best that she could. It was a release to me to know it was OK for her to make the decisions. I had to let go."

"The family—our daughters and their husbands—have been so supportive of us," said Marjorie Stiles. "How grateful we are for children who stepped in and helped.

They have been really wonderful, a blessing to us. One daughter would call every day and leave a message on the answering machine: 'Hi, Mom, I love you!' "

The patient must make the final decisions as long as he or she is able. In my situation I am blessed with three sisters who sacrificed their time, money, and family life to care for our father and help me when I needed it. Each sister lives about 2,000 miles from me. Spread across the country, we are typical of the society I mentioned above. Yet we each took our turn caring for Daddy in his own home during chemotherapy. Although each daughter wanted to have our father with her, to be his caregiver, and to enjoy his last days with their families, each sister was in favor of his decision to move in with my family. They supported my decisions while still asking the important questions and expressing their differences of opinion. But the final decisions were our father's, and he took the information, our opinions, and discussion and made up his own mind. The family support was gracious and uplifting.

When a family member visits for a few days, it is often hard for the caregiver to turn the total care over to the person who has come to help. The caregiver needs that respite, but the interdependence that has developed is hard for both patient and caregiver to let go of. In my situation I found that each of my sisters had a role to play with our father, primarily due to the differences in personalities. Each felt, however, that even though I tried to get out of the house and take a break, our father would not relinquish the total care to them. He depended on me to be in charge. It is a difficult line to walk—not to give the patient the impression that you're abandoning him or her, but at the same time taking that much-needed break. If it is at all possible for the primary caregiver to go away somewhere close by while another family member cares for the patient, it would be advisable. Just make sure that the family member has all of the necessary information and can make proper decisions. The medical log is absolutely crucial here. If a major decision needs to be made, you can return quickly or give your input by telephone. A brief vacation will work wonders for body, mind, and soul.

If your family is accustomed to praying together, *this is the time to do it!* If your family has not prayed together, or finds it awkward, *this is the time to do it!* The bonding together in prayer, with or without the patient, can bring great joy to all. And if there are any misunderstandings, it can pave the way for healing.

Respite Care

Respite care is just that—a respite from the heavy load of caregiving. It can be in many forms, and the caregiver greatly appreciates anything that gives him or her a few hours each week to go grocery shopping, go for a walk, take a break, and possibly even get a little bit of much-needed sleep. For some conditions, such as Alzheimer's disease, there are specific respite programs for the patient. And in some areas there are adult day-care centers or other activities for the patient while the caregiver takes a break.

Explore the opportunities for respite, because this could be a lifesaver in helping the caregiver avoid burnout.

Support from Friends

Friends are important during times of crises, but friends have different gifts. One can buoy your spirits; another can call and support you by saying, "I'm praying for you"; and some can cook and clean, seeing things that need doing. In our busy, frenetic world friends are not as able to be of support as in previous generations. Yet there are some who will be there when you need them.

What can others do to help? "I have learned how important it is to have someone bring in food, to send a pudding over, and to do it without asking if they can, but to just do it," said Marjorie Stiles. "My dad needed someone to come for a few hours—even two hours—each week when he was taking care of my mother with Alzheimer's. When he would go out to the grocery store, he would come back and find my mother had done something she shouldn't have done, but if he had had someone there for a short time, it would have been so helpful. I have learned that one should say, 'I am bringing food on Tuesday,' or 'I'm here to do the laundry for you,' or 'Let me go to the grocery store for you.' "

Don't allow the support or nonsupport you receive from your friends during a time of crisis to affect your ongoing friendship. Some friends know what to do, how to help, what your needs may be. And some friends don't. But if a friend asks, "What can I do?" don't say, "Nothing." It may be hard to believe people don't know how to help, but when they do offer, accept their offer graciously. Let them know that you will get back to them. Soon thereafter, give them a call with a way in which they can help— shopping for you when they go to the grocery store, taking or picking up the cleaning, sitting and visiting with the patient for a half hour while you take a break, bringing some bread or soup or another dish that would give you a break from cooking (or bringing something you could freeze to put away for the day when you have to take that trip to the emergency room and don't have time to cook). One caregiver was given a week's worth of meals for her family, to be put into the freezer and taken out as needed. What a practical help!

It may be that a friend wants to help and expresses that desire, but when you ask for help, the friend does not actually come through for you. Don't be discouraged. People are well-meaning, but priorities are not always the same for everyone. In our society discretionary time for reaching out to others is not always possible.

In some cases a friend may say, "I want to help by . . . " and tell you what they plan to do. If this is not going to be a help, you need to be gracious but let that person know that "the help I really need is. . . . " In my situation one well-meaning person offered the kind of help that I knew would upset my father. I tried to turn the suggestion to, "That is great, but it would be better if. . . . " The help, however, never materialized. You need to set the ground rules and be sensitive to the needs of the patient while trying to enjoy the help that friends might bring.

One woman offered help to a caregiver, but never actually gave it. Months after the patient had died, the woman was so guilt-ridden that it affected her friendship with the caregiver. Although the caregiver tried to be understanding, the caregiver had a hard time trusting the friendship. It's a precarious situation. Friends are wonderful and are needed during times of crisis, but the friendship should not suffer because of unfulfilled expectations. If you are a friend or relative of a caregiver, don't promise to be of help unless you are sure you will fulfill that promise.

It is often difficult when a patient must change locations and move away from friends. At the same time the caregiver must have a strong support system in order to receive what is needed, but the caregiver must remember that people will react differently than they would if it were a spouse or an immediate family member who needs care. And if it is an older parent involved, it is hard for friends to see that person as anything other than an elderly, dying patient. They don't see the patient as the vibrant, alive person he or she may be inside, the way the patient's own friends and family do. They see death and rapid decline, which can be hard on the caregiver and cause feelings of frustration.

As I am writing this book, one of my brothers-in-law has been diagnosed with extensive lymphoma and is undergoing strong chemotherapy. My sister has been trying to take up the slack and care for him and the family. She said: "I need people to call and ask how I'm doing. People have gone on with their lives. Meanwhile, the illness is old news now. They may think you have gone on too, but it was really about the fourth or fifth month that I had my hardest time. First, physically being someone you're not used to. Then you have to be emotionally strong. In addition, you're still carrying the same responsibilities you've always had, plus what the other person used to do, plus care for the other person, plus additional financial and insurance arrangements—all at once! There are bills on the floor.

"I wish that someone would come and visit us," she continued, "but people forget. It's hard to realize that the patient cannot cope with making decisions, particularly the financial ones. He hands me the bills. He does not see the scope of life. He acts like he's normal, but cannot emotionally or intellectually handle things when he's going through the worst part of chemotherapy. It's like he's in a tunnel. There are openings in the tunnel, but he cannot get a full scope. All he can handle is one thing at a time, and then only when he's feeling well." A spouse caregiver made all of these statements. She was barely keeping afloat with all of the extra responsibilities, including her own job. Her plea for help is very common and one that needs to be heard by those in her support system.

One of the great joys of my father's last months was the regular visits he received from a young woman and her preschool daughter. She came and sat with him and patted his hand. She treated him as alive and special. One time when things were very discouraging, she unexpectedly arrived at the emergency room and stayed with him while I went for a fifteen-minute break. The love between them was mutual, and she gave him respect and dignity. She brought great joy. Her visits were more helpful to me than a thousand cooked dinners or completed errands. She cared about my father. And that's the bottom line support that the caregiver wants and needs. The patient is foremost—and when the patient is loved and supported, the caregiver can breathe deeper and with more joy.

Support from the Church

This topic is very important. Unfortunately, we can barely scratch the surface. The church should take a major role in caring for the dying and the caregiver by providing the necessary support. My personal experience probably indicates the lack of understanding for the needs of caregivers by many church pastors and leaders. The caregiver should never have to ask the pastor or other church member to come and visit the patient. The caregiver should not have to ask for the Lord's Supper or other spiritual nourishment to be provided for the homebound. The church must be active and aggressive in meeting the needs of all of its members—if it is truly to be the body of Jesus Christ. It is unconscionable—to put the church member in a position of crying out to the church for help. Yet that's what happens, and in some cases, it takes time and much prayer to overcome the feelings of abandonment, because of being treated with disregard and total thoughtlessness. Indeed, both patients and caregivers feel isolated when they are treated in such a manner.

Sometimes when church members do visit the patient, they don't realize how much the patient and caregiver both need to have the spiritual support. "Not many people pray with us when they come to visit, and we really need it. Even the elders of the church" was the furtive statement of one hurting caregiver.

Caring for the members of one's church body is of utmost importance. It is equally important for the caregiver to correctly handle any anger, bitterness, or feelings of resentment toward the church, pastors, or other members for their neglect. These feelings do nothing but lead to self-destruction. In some situations, people have totally left the church because of such resentment and bitterness. As a caregiver, try to deal with these feelings as quickly as possible.

The other side of the coin is that a caregiver needs to make the needs known in the first place. This can be done with one telephone call to the church office. After which a sensitive and caring pastoral staff will follow through immediately. In some cases, churches will receive the information from a hospital. Either the church checks with the hospital admittance desk on a regular basis, or the hospital chaplain will give the church a call when a church member is admitted.

Sometimes a pastor or church visitor does not know how to make visits to a sick and/or dying person. There are some ground rules that should be followed; and if visitors don't know them, then you, the caregiver, must alert them to the facts in a gracious way: (1) Don't allow anyone who has a cold or infection of any kind into the room with the patient. (2) Keep the visits short—five to ten minutes is a good rule of thumb. (3) Don't ever sit on the bed with the patient. (4) Bring a card, a cassette tape of the service, or a church bulletin for the patient to keep him or her connected with the congregation. (5) Build a relationship by sharing what you're doing, and treat the patient as if he or she were still living. Talking about the future—death and the believer's hope—is appropriate, at the right time and in the right manner. (6) Read Scripture and pray, but don't ask the patient to pray, unless that seems to be the patient's desire.

A new position in a growing number of innovative churches is that of health minister. Because of the practical demands of spiraling health care costs, and with the goal of integrating physical and spiritual care and well-being, this holistic look at life is spreading across the nation. Churches are hiring nurses to do everything from cholesterol screenings and health and nutrition education to stress management and exercise. They are visiting shut-ins and new parents and overseeing the health and welfare needs of the congregation, including, in some cases, CPR training for the church staff and congregation.

"In their role as ministers of health, these nurses also typically deal with loss and grief, dependencies and addictions, depression, eating disorders, and dysfunctional relationships. They make referrals to appropriate agencies and resources, hold clinics to combat flu and tuberculosis, and teach classes on such topics as sex education, AIDS and bioethics.[1] A number of denominations across the country are beginning such parish programs, some in connection with local hospitals, and several universities have added specialty degrees in parish nursing: Azusa Pacific University in California; Georgetown University in Washington, D.C., and Marquette University in Milwaukee, Wisconsin.[2]

"Parish nursing and health ministry is growing in all major denominations, giving tangible help to families coping with health-related needs, including aging parents," according to Marsha Fowler, Director of the Parish Nursing Program at Azusa Pacific University. "This focus links the health care with one's faith. There are two national sources to find help in this growing field: Health Ministry Associates is an association that encompasses the church, laity, health profession, and families in the church, and assists in establishing programs on the local levels; the Parish Nurse Resource Center, Park Ridge, Illinois, is a service for nurses who want to start a health ministry within a church or hospital setting. Both will have information that might be helpful to the caregiver, to discover what is available in your area. Since such groups are beginning quite rapidly across the country, the caregiver will want to be in contact to see what is developing."[3]

The parish nurse is an excellent resource for the family in need. The nurse provides spiritual care for the caregiver and the patient. If a parish nursing program is not available in your church or community, you can go to the right pastor, the one with expertise in pastoral care and counseling, to find the helps that you need. Support groups, such as caregivers and bereavement groups, and groups who deal with special interests, such as Alzheimer's support groups, are very helpful.

Such practical programs in the church can alleviate the many feelings of frustration and abandonment that church members can experience in a caregiving situation. One of the great needs that a patient and caregiver has is to try to understand why and how to accept the pain and suffering that the believer endures and the inevitability of facing death. Many pastors, particularly younger ones, have never experienced the death of a family member, and many feel inadequate to deal with such problems. In addition, Fowler believes contemporary medicine does not allow people to deal with the inevitability of suffering. Because of technological advances in recent years, she said, medical technology is primarily focused on prolonging life regardless of its quality.

"But the painless, non-suffering life is not possible. Medicine cannot tame the terror and eliminate the darkness. Yet," she added, "parish nurses can help address this by providing unique counsel traditionally not provided either through churches or in doctor-patient relationships."[4]

What a wonderful ministry and blessing to the caregiver and patient to have such resources available from one's own church. As of the date of this article, the parish nurse movement is growing, particularly among the Evangelical Lutheran, Seventh Day Adventist, Christian Church, and Presbyterian denominations. A national organization, the Health Ministries Association based in Des Moines, Iowa, is also growing, particularly in southern California and the Midwest, and also in Virginia, Pennsylvania, Connecticut, and Michigan.[5]

Spiritual nourishment for the patient in a nursing home is important. In some homes various church groups volunteer to provide music and a church service or Bible study. This is not only often beneficial for the patient but for the caregiver as well. Doris Stephens recalled that "my favorite time to visit my mother was when a church member came each week for a Bible study with some of the residents of the nursing home. We all had something to do together, because we sang together. Mother could not talk, but she loved to sing. When a volunteer violinist or accordionist came to entertain the patients, Mother always enjoyed that, and so did I."

Much more can be said about support from the church. One important suggestion, based on my own experience, is to find at least one person whom you can call to pray for you personally. This should be a person whom you can trust, who will not talk to other people and betray confidences, and who will accept you no matter what you might say—even if you display anger toward God. This person could live at a distance with fewer telephone calls between you. But try to find such a person for your own personal, sounding-board support from within your church.

The church prayer chain is also an important support for crisis situations. Don't feel embarrassed to call and ask for prayer. That's what it's committed to do.

The hospital chaplain can be a great help for the patient. Be certain to get to know him or her and to let the chaplain know each time the patient must enter the hospital. That friendly face and a brief prayer gives a great sense of care to the patient.

Other Support Resources

Community resources vary from place to place, but most cities and towns have some kind of support group for caregivers and often for patients. The same story is often told that the caregiver waits too long to join a support group, thinking that he or she does not need one. Unfortunately, as time progresses, the need is there but the energy to invest in such a group is dissipated.

A support group can be a lifesaver. Some caregivers may be nervous about joining a support group. Don't be afraid. You will most likely find that the other members are feeling the same way as you, and it is a great comfort to have someone else say to you, "I feel the same way." These people will not try to interfere with your life, but they will become friends who can share your burden. One woman said, "We talk about the problems of caregiving and what we are going through. The problems are there. We can't take them away. But we can help each other by talking about them." Another woman, caring for her husband since he suffered a stroke, has felt like a mother or nurse, not a wife. Her sense of loss has led her to premature feelings of widowhood. In a support group she was able to admit to feelings of panic, isolation, and being trapped, because she was facing her husband's illness alone.

Support groups may sound like places for self-revelation, where one shares the deepest and most intimate secrets. But most people find them to be truly supportive — a place where they are understood, where they can be themselves and not be afraid to talk about the difficulties they're experiencing. Of course, if there are informal Christian support groups in a church or even a small group of friends, that would be ideal. The opportunity to pray with others and receive spiritual encouragement would add an extra dimension.

One word of caution: If you don't already have such a group in your community or church and you want to start one, organize it early in your caregiving experience. When you need it the most later on, it takes too much energy to try to begin one. At the time of my father's illness, there was no such group for caregivers in our community. I did manage to meet with interested leaders to ascertain the need, which I found to be quite prevalent. I had to give up the idea of starting one because I did not have the time or inner resources to organize and plan. My schedule was too erratic to take such leadership. Now, as the need is becoming more widely expressed, there are several such groups.

Often support groups are offered in community centers or in cooperation with the local hospital. They will give help by answering practical problems, raising your awareness of services that may be available to you, and bringing in specialists to answer technical medical questions. These groups can provide information about a network of help that you might be able to use. And they often offer education on invaluable ways to cope. There are many specialized support groups across the country, dealing with Alzheimer's, cancer, heart, stroke, and other diseases. Check with your local communities' resources, hospitals, and community center for a special support group for your particular situation.

Adult day-care centers are springing up across the country as places where the somewhat ambulatory patients can rehabilitate or find physical, occupational, and speech therapy. These centers provide nursing care and opportunities for socialization for many patients, particularly those recovering from stroke, heart problems, and other such illnesses. The adult day-care center offers the caregiver a respite from the burden of caregiving, and provides the patient with a source of encouragement and help for personal recuperation.

When exploring the possibilities and services available at an adult day-care center, be certain to find out if the facility is licensed and certified and what the patient to staff ratio is. (It should be one staff person to seven or eight patients, unless the patient has special needs, in which case the patient load should be fewer.)

As the population ages, more creative ways to support both the caregiver and the patient will be found. Hopefully, those Christians who have had such experiences will be able to give leadership in this area of Christian responsibility. Perhaps you may be able to spark the beginnings of such a group within your church and/or community by expressing your concerns and needs to the appropriate leaders. One person *can* make a difference.

PART THREE
Facing the Future

CHAPTER SEVEN
Home Care, Institutional Care, and Hospice Care

Older adults are projected to be a large percentage of the U.S. population during the next decade. Meanwhile, long-term care for the aging is becoming more and more of a concern. It is "unaffordable for most people — nursing home stays now average over $30,000 per year in many parts of the country. Long-term care insurance policies — many of which have significant gaps — cost some purchasers as much as $2,000 per year. Care at home, which is preferred by most people, can also be costly, depending upon an individual's needs."[1]

There are no easy solutions to the caregiving situation. What we have is the Christian's responsibility to care for those in need, and particularly for one's own immediate family. Various options should be considered; finances, personal commitments, and resources all play into the decision-making process. Placement in an out-of-home facility depends on the level of care necessary and the functional capability of the patient.

Long-term care may start with home care, and then it may need to be transferred to an intermediate care facility, where the patient is relatively independent but in need of assistance with bathing, dressing, getting out of bed, and medications. Or the patient may need twenty-four-hour nursing services that a skilled nursing facility or nursing home provides. In a growing number of cases, toward the end of one's life hospice care is a viable option that is being relied upon more and more.

Long-Term Care at Home

"I want to die at home." That's what the majority of us desire. If we were given the option, being in the comforts of our own environment would be our choice. That's the way it used to be before modern medicine. In fact, it still is in many countries. To end our days with loved ones nearby gives us a secure feeling of hope and comfort. Actually, if the truth be known, we really don't anticipate the dying process. We don't want to suffer; pain is not something we look for. Yet if we must suffer—and no one is immune to that possibility—we'd like it to be in our own surroundings with loved ones.

Home health care companies are sprouting up across the country, and many experts believe home care may answer the crisis of managing the country's health care costs. " 'The support you get from home care is tremendous,' said Dr. Mary E. Frank, President of the San Francisco-based California Academy of Family Physicians and a practicing family doctor in the Bay Area. 'The nurses go above and beyond what the job calls for.' Frank said that as the 21st Century approaches, exorbitant costs will continue to be the primary roadblock to good, universally available care."[2]

There are many agencies springing up across the country to provide the services that are needed for in-home care. Be certain that the agency is bonded, ask for references, and have a checklist of what you expect the agency to provide. The agency will even do the paperwork for you, the billing of insurance, and other such needs. They will also screen the caregivers and will assess the situation before matching the caregiver with the patient.

Many doctors and hospitals have begun to integrate

home care as an integral part of the total health care system, according to Duane Donner, president of the California Association of Hospitals and Health Care Systems.[3] There are many more options available as health professionals recognize more and more home care for the dying patient as a viable option. With the spread of AIDS, with the health care system in disarray, and with the aging of the population, new businesses are springing up that provide many services for the practical needs of the patient at home. Of course, some of these services are applicable to the nonterminally ill, who are bedridden or must receive full-time care while recuperating from illness, stroke, accident, or other major problems.

As the home health care industry provides more and more services to the long-term patient, the caregiver will have more and more helps, both with personnel and technology. Technological innovation has revolutionized the home care industry in the last decade. And more is being done. "We can do more technically without sacrificing quality. In some instances home care increases the quality of care to a patient," according to Norman Kahn, director of education for the American Academy of Family Physicians. But, according to Mike Miller, chief operating officer for Abbey Healthcare Group, Inc., Costa Mesa, California, one of the nation's largest health care service providers, only 5 percent of patients who could benefit from home health care use such services today. "Home health care is evolving hourly, daily, and weekly."[4] Readers of this book should investigate what is possible for them locally in the home care situation.

But exercise caution. When choosing health care services to be used in the home, particularly in case of infusion therapy, and if the patient is still ambulatory and able, be certain that the costs are less expensive than the outpatient visit.

The aging population will continue to create a need and market for home health care services, for those who can take care of themselves to some degree and for those who require a caregiver but who choose to stay at home. Medical services are available to patients at home for intravenous, respiratory, and rehabilitative therapies. (These include chemotherapy, pulmonary diseases, ventilator care, and routine nursing.) Some companies specialize in treatments for respiratory therapy and occupational therapy; other services are being developed. Medical devices such as "electronic drug pumps designed for exclusive home use make patients more independent, allowing nurse visits to be reduced from daily to biweekly."[5]

Relationships are built between the patient, the caregiver, and the professionals who become a lifeline of support for the at-home care. "Close relationships between health care providers and patients are more likely to develop when care is being provided in the patient's home. 'You're in their kingdom, a place where they feel more comfortable,' according to Angie Dickson, who specialized in oncology nursing. 'The real person comes out, and the likelihood of the relationship becoming more intense and intimate is greater. [The patients] share their pain and anger and grief much more openly in the privacy of their homes. You also get to know a patient's family or support system, and often get involved in supporting them to see it through to the end.' "[6]

The health care professional really cares for the patient, and has to keep a fine balance between caring too much and being helpful. "You need to set clear boundaries and remember that you're there to assist the patient in maintaining his or her health," says Jim Lacy, Director of Specialty Programs for Lifecare Solutions in Tustin, California. "You have to suppress your desire to control, and you need to respect the patient's choices, even when you may not agree with them. You also need to maintain a sense of balance between caring for others and caring for yourself."[7]

Does the patient benefit from being at home? In many cases, it is far easier for the caregiver, particularly if there are available services and others to help out when needed.

In my case, I found that I was always thankful to be home from a hospital stay. We were able to outfit my father's room with a hospital bed and bedside table, a hospital commode, oxygen, a feeding tube for the nighttime, and other equipment that were far better for my father and my family. A nurse's aide visited him three times each week for bathing and hair washing. A physical therapist came three times a week to help him exercise. And the registered nurse visited him once a week to heparinize his port-a-catheter and check him. It turned out that the R.N. actually was there more often, because we usually needed extra help, particularly toward the end. In addition, the R.N. communicated closely with physicians, sometimes on a daily basis.

Advice from an R.N. or from one of two doctors was only a telephone call away. Most of the care, however, was maintenance and I took the blood pressures, administered medication, monitored the oxygen, fixed the feeding tube for the nighttime, and assisted in bathroom help. At times I needed assurance that I was doing the right things. I also needed help in providing the correct pain medication, which was a daily adjustment. The people who were involved in care became a team, and my father appreciated and enjoyed their care and visits up until the end. The nurse in charge of his case was a Christian and provided fellowship and encouragement for both my father and me. Indeed, the home care team was a gift from God.

Home health care services offer many resources that are most convenient: speech, physical, and occupational therapy, skilled nursing assessments, home health aides for personal care, dietary consultation and evaluation, pharmacist consultation, health care cost counseling, resource referrals, patient teaching, social work, twenty-four hour on call services, and help with insurance and Medicare billing. Some home health care companies specialize in certain areas of home care, such as providing rental furniture (beds, tables, wheelchairs, walkers, pillows, etc.), dietary needs (liquid food, feeding bags and feeding equipment), and respiratory services (oxygen, etc.).

Rates for home health care are usually reasonable and are often covered by insurance. The caregiver should, however, be certain to check the references and costs to find out what is offered and what insurance or Medicare will pay. As the industry continues to expand, more and more services will be available, and the competition will increase.

Many registered nurses who have specialized in geriatrics are owners/operators of such companies, and they take personal interest in providing excellent care. Thus more than physical needs will be addressed. These small companies see the total at-home caregiving experience as being worthwhile for all involved.

Case or Care Management

When most people think of long-term care, they immediately think of nursing-home care, "but it can also mean help with housework, shopping or transportation, assistance with bathing, dressing or eating, rehabilitative care, and/or intensive skilled-nursing care. Unfortunately, the systems that deliver these services are fragmented, hard to understand and difficult to work with. Typically there is no single source for all the information and services."[8] A possible solution that is being tried is called case or care management.[9]

Care management offers help for individuals to assess their needs, and then "locates, arranges for, and monitors the required services."[10] The Care Manager is becoming a helpful service for the elderly who live far away from family and who need assistance. These services are coordinated with Area Agencies on Aging, local hospitals, social services and health departments, and private geriatric-care managers.

One such innovative program has begun in Iowa. This program is composed of thirty-two agencies in a consortium offering services for people who would otherwise require nursing-home care. It provides everything from home-health aides who clean and help shop, to lawn care, meals, a visiting social worker, emergency medical response, help with personal finances, rides to the doctor, a visiting nurse, and help getting out of bed and dressed each morning. These services and others are tailor-made to each person's particular situation. They are billed to the clients "on a sliding scale according to their income. Those with modest resources pay nothing."[11] According to Beth Riechers, coordinator of the program, most of the persons in the program "would otherwise be in a long-term care facility."[12]

More than a dozen elder care programs have been started in Iowa since 1980, according to Thomas Miskimen, director of the Heritage Area Agency on Aging. Some of these programs include a "respite-care program that trains volunteers in providing caregivers a break from their duties." In all of these programs volunteers, particularly elderly volunteers, are an important part of the program.[13] It is expected that more and more states will look to such programs as models for support-giving for the elderly, and that caregivers will be able to benefit as a result.

Care management is still in its infancy. There are no regulations as of this writing, and the costs and quality may vary. As in all choices, one should consider experience and background, and check references, as well as the caseload of such a group. "Ideally, a full-time care manager should handle no more than fifty–seventy-five clients."[14]

Be careful to check the credentials of the care manager with the National Asssociation of Private Geriatric Care Managers.[15] Before hiring a care or case manager, ask the following questions: What is your experience? Do you have a license? Do you screen service providers? Are you bonded? Do you carry professional liability insurance? Do you monitor service personally? What are your fees? Do your fees include initial assessment of the patient? Will you provide a written contract specifying services and fees?

Be certain that you do your homework. You can check

with the Visiting Nurse Association, Area Agency on Aging, doctors, and even the Better Business Bureau. The benefits of a good care manager can be very positive. (See bibliography for ordering information about care management.)

Nursing Homes

Based on my own experience, taking care of the patient at home is probably the best care option for the elderly. But we did come to a point where we were uncertain as to whether or not we could adequately care for my father if he lingered for a long time. In our situation we never had to consider seriously a nursing home, but we were prepared if the need arose. This is not the case, however, with many people. A little bit of legwork early on can save a lot of trauma and distress for the patient, the caregiver, and the family. Check out the nursing home options before you might need to make a decision. When it comes to making the decision, choices usually have to be made very quickly. They can often end up being unsatisfactory; and sometimes, the patient will even need to be moved again.

Actually, the percentage of elderly in nursing homes overall is quite low. The figures vary, but according to one reliable source, "only 7 percent of seniors over sixty-five will ever need to live in nursing homes."[16] But the fear of having to go to a nursing home is one of the greatest fears for many people as they age. The abuse and neglect that do exist in some nursing home facilities are frightening prospects, particularly if the aging person has no family or other resources to care for him or her. There is much written in the popular media, as well as in other books on aging, that will address this problem in depth. For the purposes of this discussion, we must acknowledge that some nursing homes can be places to be feared. But with good investigation and preparation, a nursing home may also be the right place for the elderly patient who needs that extra care when or if the home care situation is not possible.

Sometimes care can become so overwhelming that the health of the caregiver is also threatened. For older people in particular, caring for their spouse following a stroke or heart attack may sometimes mean that the caregiver's health quickly degenerates. One family's children found their mother to be like a time bomb waiting to go off from all of the cleaning, cooking, and personal care she provided for her elderly husband. The mother eventually suffered a heart attack, attributed in part to years of stress from constant caregiving.

For some, the good health of the caregiver may depend on the placing of one's spouse or parent in a nursing home. "Caregivers at home carry a heavy load," said Ron Shackelford. "They underestimate the amount of energy involved, and then they have a heavy guilt trip when they are not able to do it all."

This is particularly true of those caring for patients with Alzheimer's or dementia. An elderly friend of ours, whose children lived far away, cared for her husband with Alzheimer's disease for several years. For several months he was in a day-care facility a few days each week, which gave the wife some respite. But she finally had to place him in a nursing home facility nearby, because she could not handle the situation by herself and was close to burnout. She visited him daily for the remainder of his life, but was also able to better care for her own health.

The spouse or loved one who remains in the home surroundings with the knowledge that their loved one is in a nursing home feels terrible guilt and sometimes experiences emotional distress. Loneliness also becomes a problem.

The decision to place someone in a nursing home is quite often "more of an emotional decision," according to Elizabeth Isenhart, a psychiatric nurse at Keswick Nursing Home in Baltimore, Maryland." People just can't let go."[17] This is true both when the person who has been admitted is unaware of his or her surroundings (suffering from Alzheimer's or dementia) and when the person is totally aware of the situation.

Guilt, compounded by promises once made to "take care of you and never put you in a nursing home," can complicate the decision. "To release someone to an extended care facility is never easy," according to Ruth Bathauer. "It takes great courage to admit that you, as a caregiver, have done all you can for your loved one. Now that loved one's condition is such that you need to let go before your own health is damaged. Or perhaps the need is your own family, who may have been neglected as a result of your heavy involvement in caregiving. Because a caregiver tends to become so vulnerable, we again need to be reminded of an important truth: To release someone into an extended care facility does not mean the caregiver has failed. The caregiver role continues, but to a lesser degree. The role of the caregiver now is to provide that kind, loving support necessary to get through the initial period of adjustment."[18]

When a patient is placed in a nursing home, he or she may grieve the loss of home, surroundings, church and family activities, and the finality of such a move. The grieving process is to be expected, and depression may occur as well. The family will also grieve the loss, and even overcompensate by trying to see that everything is perfect for the patient. "They try to make everything right," according to social worker Sally Smith of the Keswick nursing home in Baltimore. "They try to make the nursing home not a nursing home; they try to correct every complaint. And, as a result, they kind of thwart the grieving process."

"The vast majority of nursing home patients thrive once they have adjusted," says Isenhart. "In a good nursing home, they get stimulation, they eat regular meals, and they are no longer socially isolated. It's [the family's] adjustment that is tougher."[19]

The family of a person who is institutionalized with good memory, awareness, and perception of his or her condition experiences other emotions. Family members may go to extremes in responding to the patient by trying to be certain that everything is just right, or they may pamper the patient to that point that it is difficult for the patient to adjust to the new surroundings. The nursing home decision may be one of the hardest decisions a person or family will ever have to make. Some tips that may ease the pain of making that decision are as follows: (1) Avoid making the promise: "I'll never put you in a nursing home." (2) Once your loved one is admitted, recognize his or her grief and let the patient talk about it. (3) Visit when you are comfortable with the idea and in an "up" mood. If it hurts to visit a loved one with severe dementia who doesn't recognize you, wait until you regain your emotional strength. (4) Don't overvisit. Don't become an excuse for the patient not to get involved in his or her new home. (5) When visiting a patient with dementia, keep in mind that his or her reality is not the same as yours. Go for a ride or a walk, if possible, but don't talk about something that requires the patient to use his or her memory. (6) Be an advocate for the patient, but don't overdose on a loved one's complaints. Check out the complaints, but don't try to make things perfect. An institution is not a home. (7) Don't get sucked into a guilt trip. When the patient says, "They drag me out of bed at 5 in the morning and feed me cold food," recognize this as the anger stage of grief. (8) Remember that this is not the first time you have felt guilty over the patient. If a parent or relative stirred up guilt in younger days, you may be prone to it now too. Remind yourself that you're doing your best. (9) If you take a patient home for a holiday visit, be prepared for some surprises. People with dementia, once settled in the nursing home, view it as home fairly quickly. If, after twenty minutes, your loved one starts talking about wanting to go home, he or she probably means the nursing facility. (10) Give yourself time to grieve your loss and your parent's or spouse's loss and to get over the loneliness.[20]

There are some situations where the nursing home or other long-term care facility, such as a board-and-care home, is either negligent or has a problem of some kind.

There are advocates—ombudsmen—for those in such situations who either can't stand up for themselves or have forgotten how to do so. These ombudsmen respond to complaints. In many cases, they help empower the patients and/or their families to see that changes are made. Ombudsmen make certain that the "appropriate agencies investigate and take whatever action is needed to protect the residents,"[21] particularly in cases involving abuse. In one situation an elderly woman was in fear because a night nurse had been too rough with her and an ombudsman was able to handle the situation by moving the patient. The ombudsmen can also help the family by offering advice when choosing a long-term care facility. They will guide the family through the "often complicated process of applying for government aid and finding a facility that will accept patients on Medicare."[22]

How does one choose a nursing home? The following guidelines are excerpted from a brochure published by the Illinois Council for Long-Term Care.[23] (1) Ask to see the home's license. (2) Ask to see the administrator's license. (3) Is the home Medicare and Medicaid approved? (4) What insurance plans are accepted? (5) Are there additional charges for personal laundry? Therapy? (6) Are residents allowed to furnish their own rooms? Can they have their own radios and televisions? (7) Can a husband and wife share the same room? (8) Are there restrictions on making and receiving telephone calls? (9) What are the visiting hours? (10) Are there provisions for personal banking services? (11) When was the last state and local inspection, and what were the results? (12) How often are fire drills held for staff and residents? (13) What types of recreational activities are available? (Check the schedule.) (14) Does the nursing home have an arrangement with a nearby hospital to handle emergencies? (15) Are special diets available? Is there a professional dietitian on staff, available as a consultant?

A continuing care or assisted care retirement center is also an option for older people, particularly because there are both residential and health care facilities under one roof, or in some cases, nearby. The continuing care facility offers the option for the older person who may need full-time medical care to go from one to the other, adjusting to his or her physical needs while remaining in the same location. The advantage of such a facility is that couples can stay in touch with each other, even if one needs to be in the nursing center.

As this book is being written, a close friend of our family is dying of cancer and heart failure in a nursing facility while his wife lives in their apartment in a wing of the same building. The wife is able to visit her husband many times a day, and occasionally she has been able to take him in a wheelchair to their apartment for a brief visit. It has been a relief for her to have his physical needs cared for. In this way she is able to maintain her physical strength, yet be there with him for companionship and the little details that make the end of his life filled with love.

Assisted care facilities, often a specific part of the continuing care facility, offer help with bathing, medications, hair, and other needs. They are designed for patients who might be physically disabled or ill, but don't yet need the round-the-clock medical attention of a nursing home. This kind of facility is meeting a particular need. In fact, "research says that 35 percent of the seniors in nursing homes don't belong there," according to Richard Sneed, spokesperson for Marriott's Senior Living Services" at Villa Valencia, Laguna Hills, California.[24] "Assisted living is the trend for the future because while only 7 percent of seniors over sixty-five will ever need to live in nursing homes, 23 percent will require personal care. Nursing homes are dreaded more than death by many seniors, social workers say. Moreover, nursing homes are by far the costliest kind of elder care."[25]

In the 1950s, denominations and religious groups began the first residential care facilities. Many still exist today. The older person, however, usually must be in comparatively good health to qualify. So it may not be an option

for the terminally ill person. Nevertheless, this kind of facility is worth exploring, particularly if the patient is in the
early stages of disease, and if there is a spouse involved
who is in comparatively good health.

Hospital Care

This is something that the caregiver inevitably will have to
deal with at one or many points during caregiving. Although every hospital is different, the nurses, doctors, administration, auxiliary staff, and nursing aides all set the
tone for the patient's well-being. In most cases, however,
it should be the caregiver who sets the tone for the patient. I am a firm believer that the caregiver not only must
accept this responsibility for the well-being of the patient
at home or in a nursing home facility, but also in the
hospital. My experience, as well as that of many others,
shows that in today's world of medicine it is impossible for
medical staff to see to it that everything is on an even keel.
The patient is always in jeopardy of being misunderstood
or overlooked, even in the best of hospitals with the best
doctors and nurses.

During my husband's hospitalization following his heart
attack, he stepped on a contaminated syringe needle that a
careless nurse had missed when she slung it at the trash
receptacle. In an age when such things can cause irrevers-
ible harm, this carelessness is inexcusable. In another example, after my father's last serious surgery, on his first
day in a regular hospital room following a week in the
Intensive Care Unit, one of the surgeons visited him. This
doctor, though a fine surgeon, had a rough manner about
him and was focused entirely on surgery. As he left, he
robustly slapped my father on his chest, where the cancer
had practically squeezed the life out of his lung. This
thoughtless gesture caused great discomfort to my father.
Being hit in the chest was very debilitating, and although
he did not complain, he mentioned its effects a while
later.

Again, had I not been so attentive to my father's needs during his hospitalization, there were many times when he would have not received a certain therapy, a change of position, or the comfort of a simple wetting of his dry mouth. These were due to overworked conditions and sometimes a lack of concern on the part of certain nurses. Two occasions in particular caused me great alarm. I relate them here so that other caregivers can learn from my experiences and hopefully see that their loved ones have the best care.

The first incident occurred when I visited my father late one night and found him in restraints. I immediately called the nurse and learned that she was an "agency" nurse, not a member of the regular night staff. Because my father had felt well enough to sit up, he had tried to do so and became dizzy. The nurse, seeing that he was elderly, made the decision to put him in restraints. She did not take the time to talk with him about it. If she had, she would have realized that he could see for himself he should not have attempted to sit up. She might simply have told him not to try again without assistance. His mind was quite capable, and he could learn from his mistake. Indeed, he would not have tried again. The situation did not warrant the ultimate indignity of putting restraints on him. When I arrived and saw him, he was very frightened and scared. I was immediately able to see to it that the restraints were removed, and I let the nurse know that under no conditions was she to allow this to occur again without first checking with my father and me, and the doctor.

This brings up the issue of restraints, which I feel is important enough to mention here. According to Steven Miles, M.D., on the NBC television program, "Dateline," 90 percent of restraints could be removed from elderly patients. In fact, restraints are used for "staff convenience," particularly in nursing homes, because there are not enough staff members to "walk the residents."[26] It is the patient's right to sign a release form not to be restrained. Indeed, it is Federal law to receive a doctor's order and written permission to use restraints.

The second incident is much like the first. I arrived early one morning to find that my father had slipped far down in his bed. He could not adjust the bed, call the nurse, or do anything to help himself. Again, the fear in his eyes still haunts me. It was horrible to know that, again, an "agency" night nurse had simply been too busy to check on him and see to it that he needed help. In this situation I strongly suggested that a directive be recorded for each shift: someone was to check him regularly during the night. I also wanted a written record that I was very upset at the incident.

The caregiver must be strong and courageous. He or she must see to it that the best care is given, even if it means going to the administrator of the hospital nursing staff or another top official. What is hard to accept is that in so many other cases this is the way the elderly are cared for, and they have no one to step in and speak for the dignity they deserve as human beings. The situation is worsened for those who are mentally alert and aware of the situation in which they find themselves.

When the caregiver is able, I suggest getting to know the hospital staff. Build relationships with the head nurse on the various shifts, the chaplain, and any administrators who are available. Let them know both your concerns and your support of them and the hospital. It is important to become a part of the hospital network so that in the event you might need extra help or information, you already have established this informal relationship.

Board and Care Facilities

Board and care homes — residences in local neighborhoods where a few patients can be housed in a home-like setting — are being started across the country. The state licenses these homes which provide a family-like setting for patients. The patients are housed either in private or semi-private bedrooms, and they become a part of a family.

They are usually designed for patients who are somewhat ambulatory but need supervisory care.

Ron Shackelford performed pastoral calls on convalescing seniors when he formulated a vision for Oceanair Manor, a home to provide for the needs of the total person. "Caregiving is a tough love situation," he said. "Choosing to put a loved one into a nursing home or board and care home is making a decision for the welfare of all concerned. A board and care home is a place that provides more of a personal touch than an institution. Caregivers are able to give personal attention to physical needs, as well as to other needs of the patient. Patients want to know that someone cares about them. They do not want a profound theological discussion, but to deal with the practical Christian living issues. They are dealing with loss, a sense of grief at their failing physical and mental capacities."

Oceanair Manor Board and Care facility is an example of the many homes that are being started. It has five rooms and five patients. Patients receive twenty-four-hour care. Each primary caregiver works a three-and-one-half-day shift each week. The primary caregiver is there twenty-four hours a day. He or she cooks the meals, does the laundry, and gives medications. An assistant comes every day from 7:30 A.M. until 1:30 P.M. to help exercise the patients, to interact with them, and to assist the primary caregiver with the cleaning, laundry, and other duties. Afternoons are quiet. The caregiver and patient will sit, talk, and watch television together. The pastor/owner visits regularly.

Quality and individual care is provided as more and more board and care homes are being started across the country. As with any similar facility, references and facilities should be thoroughly checked out before placing a patient in such a home.

Palliative Care

The goal of palliative care is to control symptoms such as pain, nausea, weakness, and weight loss. Palliative care treats the patient as a holistic person, dealing with social, psychological, and spiritual needs as well as with the physical. Many doctors are beginning to realize that palliative care for the terminally ill is crucial, and that this care is possible with at-home care or even in a nursing home, but it fits most naturally with the hospice.

Although palliative care has been primarily associated with hospices, many predict that by the year 2000 it will be a "mainstream medical specialty with professorships, postgraduate training programs, and departments in major medical centers." The first postgraduate programs are at the Cleveland Clinic, M.D. Anderson Cancer Center in Houston, Texas, and in association with the Hospice at the Texas Medical Center.[27]

Cancer cures are slow in coming. Instead, the number of incidences is rising. With the aging of the U.S. population, more diseases will also be prevalent. Many doctors are recommending aggressive medical treatments, such as chemotherapy and radiation, when the time might be better focused on palliative care—pain control and the other needs that will give some quality of life as the end nears.

As oncologists realize that palliative care is important to the patient, the situation may change, according to Stuart A. Grossman of the American Society of Clinical Oncology. Grossman, chairman of that organization's committee on cancer pain, says, "There has been too much emphasis on treatment and not enough on palliative care. We need to learn to pay more attention to the little things that mean a great deal to the patient."[28] Some patients, having tired of treatments, particularly chemotherapy, ask for palliative care just to be comfortable. "The growing interest in euthanasia is partly a result of doctors' failure to address the needs of the terminally ill. If more hospitals and clinics adopted palliative care programs to address pain and other symptoms, the fear of dying and the appeal of euthanasia would lessen," says Martin Skinner, president of the Academy of Hospice Physicians.[29]

How thankful I am for the doctors who attended my

father. With the exception of one, all believed in palliative care. They listened and understood the needs of the whole person, and they were understanding of life and death. And how grateful we can be to God for the believers who are in the medical profession, for those kind and understanding doctors who treat the dying with love and dignity!

When Elizabeth Strauch, the first to train in palliative care at M.D. Anderson Cancer Center, changed her specialty from plastic surgery to palliative care, she did so against the advice of many. She says helping terminally ill patients during the last few weeks and months of their lives is "my concept of what a real doctor was about: sitting at the bedside, listening to the patient, and making them feel better. That's gotten lost in the aggressive treatments, the high tech, the big business. It's one of the last bastions remaining of old-time medicine—gentle, contemplative, and caring."[30]

Hospice Care

The hospice provides care for the dying, either in the patient's home or in a hospice location. The hospice treats the patient and supports the family through the last days of life and during the bereavement. Only those patients who have the doctor's verified prognosis that life is deteriorating and there is a short amount of time to live qualify for a hospice. The hospice programs, which were begun outside of hospitals, are becoming more well known, both to physicians and patients. Even so, "few hospital-based doctors have daily contact with such programs, and medical students receive little exposure to palliative care practitioners."[31] Only a few of the nation's hospice programs are in hospitals. Most either contract with hospitals or accept referrals from them. Some private doctors are suggesting palliative care and hospice care, but for many doctors it means a loss of income and ignorance of what this kind of care has to offer. Often doctors do not know how to talk about dying, as was the experience in my father's case early in his diagnosis.

"Several trends in our contemporary society cause the care of terminal patients to move from the traditional family setting to a residential hospice," according to Paul Van Oss, President of the Board of Directors of Home of Hope Hospice in Grand Rapids, Michigan. "These trends include the greater number of single families; increased mobility causing children and parents to often live hundreds of miles from each other; longevity of life with the resultant effect of increasing numbers of persons simply outliving their caregivers; and alienation from family support brought on by stigmatized disease such as AIDS. These reasons cause a major gap in our health care system, which means that terminal illness carries with it the devastating sentence of loneliness and despair. Large numbers of Americans die alone and often in much pain." Van Oss also said, "Sometimes the physical demands of an illness are greater than loved ones can meet, so an institution is the alternative. Although fully capable of meeting a patient's physical requirements, these facilities cannot begin to address the emotional or spiritual needs of a terminally ill person. It is for this reason that Home of Hope exists."

Home of Hope can be a model for other Christian hospices across the country. It was formed as a coalition between denominations, churches, and social services, and is distinctly Christian in its outlook. It is a home, a residence, which offers medical, physical, emotional, and spiritual care for the patient. And it provides comfort and help for the family of the dying.

The hospice helps the patient with the physical and emotional pain of dying. It plays a key role for many in receiving palliative care, although many patients can and do receive this kind of care at home or in a nursing home. The palliative care concept is versatile. Most often a hospice is associated with a warm, friendly place where one can go during the last few weeks or months of life, and where care for the total person will be administered.

Adult Day Care

Adult day care is a program that provides health and social services in a supervised and comfortable setting. The focus and purpose of adult day care is to prevent premature institutionalization and possibly avoid the need for nursing home care. The programs provide independent activities and personal care to meet individual patient's needs. Some programs are specialized for illnesses such as Alzheimer's disease, or other specific problems. Adult day care offers weekday programs, with some weekend offerings. Generally, centers provide morning and afternoon snacks and a lunch. There is medical and rehabilitative therapy available as well. Some centers even provide transportation.

Whatever care your loved one will need, be certain that your love and care is above all shown to the patient in an ongoing way. Let the patient know that you are there to support him or her, and to provide security and oversight for the best possible care during this difficult time of life.

CHAPTER EIGHT
Facing Death

"They, then, who are destined to die, need not be careful to inquire what death they are to die, but in what place death will usher them." St. Augustine.

We are not afraid of death itself. We are frightened by the actual process — the event of dying. Although for Christians "to die is gain,"[1] death itself will never cease being our "last enemy."[2] Death is not something that we as humans enjoy thinking about. This is true for the patient who must face mortality and impending death. And it is true for the caregiver who must face grief for the patient and inevitably his or her own death in the future. Emotions are mixed; grief is mingled with the believer's hope. The confidence of eternal life brings underlying peace and contentment, mixed with the fear of the unknown. John Calvin said it well: "We die, but in dying, we pass over into life."

The caregiver has a wonderful opportunity to remind the Christian patient of the hope that is his or hers as a believer in Jesus Christ as personal Savior. For some people, facing death is a time to reflect and take an accounting of what has been accomplished during life. Some may look back and see wasted years, years spent out of communion and relationship with family and even with God.

The forgiveness from God that is the believer's is right there for the asking, and the caregiver may be in a position to remind the patient of this truth. The following experience with forgiveness was shared with me in a friend's letter as I was thinking about this chapter. The names and identities have been changed.

> We've had almost no personal contact with Jim for eighteen years. He was in our Christian group during university, and he was a strong believer. We had heard he was single, gay, and living in a large city. We could have looked him up any of the many times we were in his state, but we didn't for various reasons, mostly related to his homosexual lifestyle and value system. The avoidance was probably mutual. One day, however, a mutual friend let us know that he was ill, so my husband and I decided to visit him.
>
> We later learned it was the first and last day he was voluntarily dressed and out of bed. We went to close out our friendship or something. I was totally unprepared for the overwhelming rush of love I felt for him. He had been so special to me in college — not romantically — but as a brother, spiritual comrade, kindred spirit, confidant, and I realized in one instant that he was still the same person I had loved before. Naturally, this emotion caused some confusion within. I was at the same time repulsed by homosexuality in general, but flooded with a desire to nurture and care for him. Perhaps our different lives could not have withstood colliding until now. They did not in fact collide, but more merged.
>
> I wrote to him after my husband and I returned home. After all, if a dying man can use anything, it's probably the love of people he knows. I shared my conflicting emotions with him and reminded him of the shared times we had experienced that were but memories of half of our lifetime ago. I also offered to take a week or so as caregiver, which I sincerely

meant but did not expect him to take me up on. I did, however, expect him to somehow accept my eleventh-hour expression of love and concern as genuine, and I told him that, and he did.

I also wrote to some other old mutual friends, spread out across the country, who had not heard of his illness. What began to occur then is that Christian friends out of the past, all of whom had been "divorced" from Jim lo these many years, began to call or visit. And Jim began to feel loved. And he began to feel nudged and called by God, as well.

Several weeks went by. We talked on the telephone, and he urged me to write again. I sensed a hunger for God and a yearning in him that I dared to write back and acknowledge him. In the meantime, a family member suggested that since he believed my love for him, I had to take it one step further and remind him of the truth concerning sin and forgiveness that he once knew. As she said, I had nothing to lose, and he was facing eternity. I did not want to write such a letter, but the Lord made it both easy to know what to write and impossible not to write it. For a short time every sermon, Sunday School class, and Bible study I attended pointed in some way to the contrast between darkness and light, the need for forgiveness, the prevalence of sin, and our longing to deny sin as sin.

I wrote the letter. I thought it might sever personal contact between us, but maybe, just maybe, the Lord would begin speaking to him, reminding him of what he knew of Him long ago. Jim was extremely touched by the letter and began to pray with Christian family members, who by this time were beginning to gather as his time seemed short. He showed the letter to various people, I think, asking—begging—them to follow up on the things I had said.

Jim scrawled out a letter to me from his hospital bed, inviting me to come and visit, acknowledging a deep longing for God's forgiveness, but saying he felt there must be a task or penance he must perform to atone for ignoring God for so long. After some heart-searching, I was on the plane the next morning and spent five days in the hospital with him. He was weak and slept a lot, but we did talk some, more from his candidness and unguardedness than because I had any great wisdom to impart.

Even though I was only part of the caregiving process for such a short time, the experience touched me profoundly. Reading a book on AIDS (*The AIDS Caregiver's Handbook*, St. Martin's Press) afterward showed me that my experience was not so unique after all, which was almost a relief to me—for it was unique for me. I have never loved anyone more than I did Jim in those few days. Holding his face, his head, his hands, his feet, and having him look at me and say, "I love you so much" gave me an uncanny picture of God's pleasure in our resting in His arms, looking into His face and saying, "I love you so much."

When I started out, I only knew that I must go; I also did not know exactly why I was going. It became quickly apparent to me that the Lord had sent me to love Jim, not to figure out long-term care, not to give him some magic words of wisdom that would set his life in order, not to preach, not even to provide physical care, although I did that too. What I said to him I barely even remember, though we repeatedly talked primarily of spiritual things in an ongoing conversation over the four to five days. I may have—by my love, which obviously went beyond the scope of shared experiences twenty years ago—given him some kind of permission to make his peace with God and to see God's grace in its raw, unmerited form.

I realized that what I had read in the book on AIDS about the incredible sharing between the dying person and caregiver is true. While the caregiver is obviously making a tremendous sacrifice and giving time and love in visible ways that people can see and respect even if they don't understand, the caregiver receives gifts from the dying person—trust and love of a kind rarely experienced, and the dying experience itself. I have read that "death is the most intimate experience of a person's life." If this is possible among strangers and non-Christians, how much more powerful when the care-er and care-ee share the hope possible only in Christ.

I was a caregiver for such a short time and really in such an undemanding, shallow way; yet I am changed. My personal, close relationships experienced a renaissance. I did not seek this, and I feel I must not boast of it, because I did not earn it in any way—it too is a gift."[3]

This letter has powerful content, and the response of the short-term caregiver is significant. Truly, being with the loved one as they face death is a most moving, life-changing and beautiful experience. I too had dreaded that day. Would I know what to do? Would it be so awful that I would be forever negatively affected by it? I had seen my husband experience his heart attack; and the convulsions and full arrest when his heart stopped were frightening. Would the death of one who is diseased and dying a slow death be equally as difficult?

Each situation is quite different. Some patients are experiencing great discomfort, and many are sedated so that they die peacefully, not fully cognizant of their surroundings. Yet the one thing that is repeated again and again by those who deal with death and dying is that when a patient is loved and cared for and surrounded by loved ones, it is much easer to face.

When my father was close to death, he said, "I can't let go." My reply was, "Let go of what, Daddy?" He replied, "Of whatever's holding me." The words came out of my mouth, undoubtedly prompted by the Holy Spirit: "Just relax in God's arms and He will hold you." My father sighed and nodded his head at the same time—a deep sigh from his whole body, and then he slowly went to be with his Lord during the next several hours. I had a tape of quiet hymns playing in his room, and the family came and went, stopping to pray with him, to tell him we loved him, and lightly touching him to let him know of our presence. He acknowledged us, and then quietly and peacefully left this earth.

It was almost hard to know that my father was dying. I sat with him off and on, each time telling him I loved him. He would nod in reply. Being with him at death, as he faced the Lord he had served so faithfully for almost a lifetime, was precious. The Holy Spirit indeed ministered to him, and comforted us, and was truly present in our midst.

My family's experience does not seem to be the exception. The following account by a daughter-in-law of her mother-in-law's death in many ways parallels ours:

When I stood by [Mom's bedside] I marveled at how little was left of the strong, capable woman I had met thirty years ago. . . . I dreaded her dying but longed for her suffering and our helpless watch to be over.

As a Christian, I wasn't afraid of death, but I was frightened by the process. I had never seen anyone die and was relieved that the doctors and nurses would be with Mom at the end. I was a little ashamed of my eagerness to get away, but there was something in Mom's eyes— riveted on mine—that held me. Perhaps it was a reflection of my own fear, and I heard myself say, "Do you want me to stay?"

Her eyes brightened. Her hand gripped mine more tightly. With a sinking feeling I said, "We won't leave you, Mom. We'll be right here till God takes you home. I promise." Her eyes shone, and I felt calmer, almost expectant, now that I had made the commitment.

Mother was in and out of a coma for the next several days. Meanwhile, two family members were always at her side. They took turns reading her favorite psalms and prayers, singing the hymns she loved.

On the third day came a moment I'll never forget. As I looked into Mom's eyes, I saw a light and love unlike anything I've experienced. From unknown depths in me came a joyous unspoken response that knit our hearts together. We seemed to exchange all the love we had wanted to share, the reconciliation of differences we had longed for. My fear of being present when she died left me in that hour. The hospital room was no longer cold and alien, but had become a sanctuary. I didn't want to leave, even for a few minutes. When painful spasms racked Mom's body, I could hold her and say with deepening conviction, "God's arms are around us, Mom. Sink into His love. He'll carry you home."

Mom's breathing was light. She was resting peacefully, I thought, like a child falling asleep in her mother's arms. The room was quiet, and time stood still as we watched. Imperceptibly she slipped from life to death — or was it the other way around? Was this the shadowland, and was she entering light and real life? Our minister put the experience of my being there in perspective when he said, "That was Mom's last gift to you." I had thought we were sacrificing sleep, battling exhaustion, suffering something of her pain. But she was the giver, and we were immeasurably enriched by her gift. We felt a closeness to her and to each other, as if we had experienced a bonding more than a parting. We grieved, but not with the anguish of losing someone without sharing their last moments. And we shared a resolve not to turn from such a gift again.

Death itself has lost something of its sting for me. One day I'll be the one to go, and I hope someone will be there to hold my hand. It will be my last gift to them.[4]

Death separates us from all that we know — creation and

the beauty of the world. It separates families, parents and children, husband and wife, friend and friend. It sometimes even makes us wonder whether God Himself is abandoning us. Death and the threat of death are overwhelming when the dying do not know the relationship that comes from a loving God. But because of the resurrection of Jesus Christ, the terror of death can be overcome. Because Christ died for us, we no longer need to fear death. Instead, we have the hope of eternal life. Because Christ was raised from the dead and now lives, we too can have that eternal life. And with that hope of life eternal, we can comfort the dying and the grieving through God's love. Because God cared for us, we in turn can love and care for others with the hope of the believer.

The death of a child, no matter what the age, is probably the hardest earthly separation. Only recently, dear friends have lost their twenty-eight-year-old son in a diving accident. Several years ago a young friend of twenty-one died during heart surgery. Another close friend lost a sixteen-year-old son in a motorcycle accident caused by a drunk driver. God has spared us from this kind of death in our immediate family, but we have sorrowed with our close friends as they have mourned and faced the great void through the years following their children's premature deaths. The pain, the struggle, the hurts, and the uncertainties are unbelievably deep, and the effects on the surviving family are life-changing. Marsha Fowler of Azusa Pacific University said, "Life transitions—the aging process, loss, declining health, illnesses, disease, trauma—any life event without joy, always raises questions that pertain to one's faith. These questions deal with either the goodness of God on one end, or the shaking of one's faith on the other end of the spectrum. The two types of questions that arise deal with the ethics of the world—God's justice, and God's fairness—one's relationship to God when dealing with a family of a dying child. Questions arise, such as, 'Is it ethical to unplug life support?' or 'How can this happen to us? This isn't fair!' "

We cannot understand God's ways, and the death of a child to disease or illness is one of those things in life that truly cannot be understood. Joe Bayly said in his book *The Last Thing We Talk About,* "We have lost three children: one at eighteen days, after surgery; another at five years, with leukemia; the third at eighteen years, after a sledding accident complicated by mild hemophilia. We don't own our children; we hold them in trust for God, who gave them to us. The eighteen or twenty years of provision and oversight and training that we normally have, represent our fulfillment of that trust. But God may relieve us of the trust at any time and take our child home to His home."[5]

The peace of the dying believer is a gift from God, particularly if that person is spiritually prepared to die. Even if the suffering and misery of disease is present, there is the underlying peace of the believer. And in the case of the terminally ill, there is time to reflect on one's life and receive forgiveness. Are we afraid to die? No. Are we sometimes fearful of what it will be like to die? Yes. But the fear can be released to the God who created life and allows death, and who sustains the patient and the caregiver as we anticipate the unknown, struggling to relax and trust in the hope of the Christian which is eternal life.

John Claypool, the Baptist minister, wrote about the Christian's hope soon after the death of his young daughter from leukemia. One thing that is "so significant to me about the biblical God is what He did about pain and evil. He not only watched His child suffer; He brought Him through it, even death! He took the pain and gathered it up unto His purpose! The raising of Christ Jesus from the dead is not only the greatest deed of the Bible; it is our basis of hope in the midst of tragedy.[6]

In his wonderful book *Heaven,* Joe Bayly said, "My courage is Christ. My hope is Christ and the door to heaven He flung open by His own death for my sins, my hope His resurrection . . . death is deliverance to life beyond your imagining . . . I may not long for death, but I surely long for heaven."[7]

Facing death is awesome, but one need not face it alone. God promises to comfort us and give us the courage to "walk through the shadow of the valley of death" . . . and to be with us. "Surely goodness and love will follow me all the days of my life, and I will dwell in the house of the Lord forever."[8]

The funeral for the believer is a time to reflect on the patient's life, to rejoice that the loved one is no longer suffering and is indeed in God's presence. Even though we can't understand that, we are thankful. But as human beings we need to have this time to sorrow and be bolstered by family and friends, who will cry and express sorrow with us. A funeral service can be a special celebration of God's faithfulness to this one person's life, and all of the people attending can be encouraged by it and can grow from seeing how faithful God is to the believer.

Marjorie Stiles said, "Mother's funeral was such a special time of testimony to her life, full of the music that she had loved throughout the years. She enjoyed the music, even during the times when she was not always aware of what was happening around her, so this was a special time of remembrance for all of us."

A funeral is also a time for families to be together. Emotions go from the highest to the lowest, from tears to laughter, and that's all right. Joy and peace blend to become sorrow, which we need to express. We can glorify God for His faithfulness and answers to prayer.

The transition from earthly life to heavenly, eternal life is God's gift to the believer through Jesus Christ's death. We as human beings cannot understand this miracle. We can only take comfort and embrace our life, knowing that we too will enjoy the fulfillment of the hope of the Christian.

PART FOUR
Caring for the Caregiver

CHAPTER NINE
Take Care of Yourself

Take care of yourself. I'm most concerned about you. How many times had I heard those words, then resolutely said to myself, "I want to take care of myself, but when and how?" Of course I wanted life to be normal, but how could I manage anything else in addition to what I was already doing? Though I knew intellectually that it was extremely important to care for my own needs, emotionally I could not even think about it. Besides, it takes time to make the time. And time had me by the throat.

It is always easier to look back on a situation; retrospect offers the opportunity to learn and evaluate, to wish we had done things differently. But when we're in the midst of a crisis, an all-consuming situation such as the demands of caregiving, how do we adjust our focus? Looking back on a few examples from my caregiving experiences has made me realize that if and when I am in a similar situation, I'll try to do some things differently. One example is the time my father arrived home from the hospital in an ambulance just before he died. I went to the driveway to meet him, trying to be upbeat. I'll never forget the look in my father's eyes; they were questioning, showing some fear and a sense of abandonment by me.

I had stayed home that morning feeling exhausted and

overwhelmed, and our daughter had gone early to the hospital in my place. I was close to caregiver's burnout. I sensed that my father was going to have days of discomfort and suffering ahead, and there was really nothing left to do but keep him comfortable. The cancer had metastisized to vital organs, and life is uncertain when that happens. I knew it could be many days of bedridden, round-the clock care for him. So I took a two-hour respite. It was luxurious. I slept through the night for the first time in weeks and took my time getting up and showering. I also had time to prepare his room so it would be comfortable and attractive when he returned from the hospital later that day.

Beth Ann spent the morning at the hospital with her grandfather, attending to those needs that the nurses did not have time for — wetting his mouth with a sponge, adjusting his bed, calling the nurses (he was too weak to do that at this point), answering the phone, caring for his personal hygiene, and the other simple activities of daily living that we take so much for granted. Thus when he was released earlier in the day than expected, Beth Ann checked him out of the hospital in my place. It was the first time that I had not been there to do this function for him during the many times he had been hospitalized, and his body language and attitude when he returned home showed me that he felt I was letting down in his care. He did not try to make me feel guilty. Since he did not want to be a burden to me, however, he deducted that my not being there with him and for him that morning meant I was beginning to feel too burdened. Rightly or wrongly, I took the guilt for that upon myself.

I had prepared for friends and nurses to begin sitting with him during the night, to sleep in his room and be there when he needed help. This too was taken as a signal to Daddy that his care was too much for me. And the last thing my father wanted was to be a burden. Wasn't that why he lived alone at a distance from family for so long? In addition to my creeping symptoms of burnout, I began to feel guilty.

What could I have done to avoid his dependence on me and me alone? How could I have avoided such possible feelings, both for my father's understanding and my reactions of guilt? Looking back, I feel that talking about the future possibilities and options would have helped the situation. After all, by this time patterns were set and he was too ill to understand just how all-consumed I had become with his caregiving. I willingly had taken on more and more time commitment, and I did not have a balance to keep my own health and welfare in focus.

Caregiver Burnout—Listen and Learn from Others

It is impossible to have exact knowledge of the specific details and to plan for what is ahead for the caregiver and patient. That's probably the hardest thing to deal with. We just can't plan our last days. But we can gain insight from others if we will listen. Since my experience I have learned, first of all, that my situation was neither unique nor isolated. I had never thought about caregiving before I was thrust into the situation, and once there, I did not have time to talk with others and find out what they had gone or were going through. Many caregivers were just beginning to share the lessons they learned to help others cope and understand. In fact, as the population ages and we live longer, the situation will continue to be addressed with helps and coping mechanisms.

"The one thing I would tell a caregiver is to take care of self before you take care of the patient," Ron Shackleford said from his experience with the elderly. "Nurture yourself, or you will burn out. I know of a wife of an Alzheimer's patient who is caring for her husband at home, and is running herself down and will be sick, working herself to the limit. She feels that she knows and understands her husband better than anyone else can. And she's probably right. But she doesn't realize what she is doing to herself. Love is not always logical. I believe that God's way is to take care of oneself, pray a lot, rest, and eat well."

Another warning signal for the caregiver is when physical exhaustion begins to take its toll on you. "Sleep deprivation is probably the number one problem for caregivers," according to Elizabeth Brown, gerontology specialist. "Also there is a need for respite care, which is probably the hardest thing to find. Keeping a schedule, trading off times of caregiving with other people, finding support from the church or community group and friends, these are all important." Another caregiver said, "Just going shopping is a problem. You don't have the ability to even think. You want to forget the kids, and Christmas."

Caregiving is a privilege. But it is also one of the most difficult things that a person will ever do. Looking back, what would or could I have done differently? Why do I want to spare our children what I experienced? Why am I investigating nursing home insurance for myself and my husband? These are all questions that need to be answered. How can you, in a caregiving situation now, avoid some of the difficulties that others have dealt with? I didn't actually experience burnout, but I came close enough to see that the experience certainly had an effect on me that bears lasting marks.

An extreme case of burnout occasionally will lead to desperation on the part of a caregiver, particularly in the case of the long-term terminally or chronically ill. For example, in Santa Ana, California, in April 1992, a woman in her late sixties doused her terminally ill husband, a wheelchair-bound cancer patient, with rubbing alcohol and set him on fire. She did this because he ate her chocolate Easter rabbit, and it inflamed her anger, ostensibly caused by caregiver burnout. "While the plight of this woman, now charged with attempted murder, was unusual in its severity, 'caregiver burnout' isn't," according to Mary Watson, an administrator at the University of California, Irvine, School of Medicine's program in geriatric medicine. "People do bizarre things when they're caregivers and burned out. And you don't know what can happen."[1]

Social workers, doctors, and other health providers say

anyone tending a seriously ill, elderly person can be driven to desperation. Their reactions, some experts on senior citizens say, can range from depression to complete physical exhaustion. In some instances, the stress has led to murder of a spouse and then suicide."[2]

Another scenario that we hear about all too often is of the elderly person who cares for a terminally ill spouse. The caregiver becomes so involved giving care that his or her own personal health, hygiene, and demeanor deteriorates, and that caregiver becomes a victim of caregiver burnout. I've known cases where the caregiver died before the patient and the patient ended up being admitted to a nursing home for a number of years following the caregiver's death. It's self-defeating to allow oneself to reach that point, but it happens for one reason or another. If you have the potential of being in such a situation, find respite care and the help that you need to avoid such a predicament.

Often caregivers will continue to push themselves to the limits, even though their personal life is deteriorating, because they have made a promise to "never place the loved one in a nursing home." There are certain promises that I have learned never to make or accept, and this is one of them. Even though my own experience was positive, I have made it clear to our children that they must not take the potential caregiving for me as a day-to-day obligation if it would be a hardship and cause personal harm to them or to their families. When the caregiver is at risk in some way, a nursing home would be the wisest and best alternative, as painful as that decision might be for the caregiver and the patient. The caregiver must realize that his or her life will go on after caregiving, and that the patient would not wish the caregiver to live a less than full life.

Social workers see a lot of caregiver burnout, according to Donna Farris, oncology social worker at Saddleback Memorial Medical Center near Leisure World (a retirement community) in Laguna Hills, California. Caregivers "may not realize the pressure they are under." At a recent work-

shop Farris conducted, she found that "some spouses con-
cur that the grueling demands of tending an ill person at
home can make them angry or physically ill."[3]

It must be pointed out again here that there are resources available to help, and with each day that passes,
more and more sources of aid are being organized.
Churches, doctors, social workers, community centers,
and a variety of agencies offer help for caregivers. It is well
worth the time to make a few telephone calls and see what
support groups and support systems are within your community. If you have not reached the point of needing such
services, plan ahead. Too often the caregiver waits until
the patient's condition has deteriorated so much that a
nursing home is the only alternative, particularly in the
case of Alzheimer's patients.

I would not change the fact that I took care of my father.
I am glad I was able to give him care. It was a rich experience, an opportunity to spend time with him and reach
out in love. This helps a person grow and develop into
being more like Christ, to identify with what it means to
sacrifice and give freely of oneself. Bonnie Genevay, a Se-
attle-based counselor and consultant, says, "When we care
for children, the satisfaction is they grow up and become
independent. But when we care for someone older, most
of the time, they will decline and die, and the satisfaction
is that we are the ones who grow."[4]

What I would change about my experience is that I
would care for myself, both physically and socially. Since I
did not continue regular physical exercise or look out for
my health, I have paid for that following his death. I also
became so isolated from other people that it has taken
many months to reenter the world, to socialize and enjoy
being with people.

Social Isolation

I first realized how far out of touch with the real world I
had become at the Christmas event my husband and I

attended. It was the only time I had been of out the house, except for doctor and hospital visits, for many months. I did not feel like talking, and I had nothing to say but to answer questions about my father (and I didn't want to go into too much detail). So I found a corner of the room and sat there, trying to just be a "mouse in the corner." What I really wanted to do was sit and cry. I was so overwhelmed to be in a social setting that I was totally out of sync.

I had lost my self-identity. I was now solely a caregiver. I had so completely immersed myself in my caregiving that I had little time for my husband, for my other family members, or for myself. Although my family was unusually understanding and supportive, this was not a healthy balance of who and what I was and am. How could that have been changed? Possibly by finding that support group or other person who had been through it already. By talking with those who had walked in my shoes and who could share with me and help me understand that I needed to keep my life in balance and take care of myself for my own sake.

Burnout sometimes becomes so problematic that people need to take time to recover from caregiving and the demands of soul and self. I can relate to the person who calls herself a "recovering caregiver": Bonnie Genevay, who cared for a mother suffering from Alzheimer's disease, "urged those for whom caregiving has become a twenty-four-hour job to 'drop the mask' when people ask how they are and tell the truth. Instead of saying 'I'm fine,' admit, 'I'm barely treading water' or 'I'm feeling very helpless,' she advised. Without that kind of honesty, caregivers risk becoming too exhausted to enjoy the rewards of giving."[5]

Because caregiving is so demanding physically, emotionally, and spiritually, one is drained of all resources and the reason for which one is giving care. To show love and concern and to be there for your loved one becomes second place. Yet above all, according to Genevay, "A loving relationship is more important than any physical caregiving we do."[6]

How Have I Changed?

When I see an elderly person being pushed along in a wheelchair, a lump fills my throat and a video instantly replays in my mind. I remember how difficult it was to be so dependent on another being, to have to be subjugated to a lesser position when you're used to being a "gentleman" and holding the elevator door, for example. I think of the pain that such a person must be enduring, and yet how that chair is a taste of freedom from a bed and a room. I try to make eye contact with the person and elicit a smile or a response. Before I would have avoided this connection so as to lessen the other person's embarrassment. Now I try to visualize the chair-bound as vigorous, strong, and healthy. And when I see an elderly person riding in the front passenger seat of a car, I realize how the loss of one's independence is a major step toward decline of health and inner resources. I wonder if the driver is sensitive to the other person's needs.

I don't want my children to have to care for me. But on this subject I feel strong ambivalence, because my daughter feels that is part of being family. So on the one hand, I don't want her to carry a load and have her life drastically altered. On the other hand, I know the joy that caregiving can bring, and I would not want to deprive her of the joy of giving. I hope that before too much time passes, we will reach a compromise plan for my own future—possibly a certain time when the plan should include the option of a nursing home.

I have learned not to be afraid to ask questions. Whether a professional is a lawyer, doctor, or other medical personnel, I don't take what a professional might say as the final answer. We were blessed to have mostly outstanding doctors. But the ones who were the most outstanding were those who were honest and did not demand that "this is the only and right way." The one doctor who was arrogant and had all of the right answers was the one who would not listen to important data and made a rash mistake, one that could possibly have stolen months of my father's life. Had this doctor listened, my father most certainly would have avoided a tremendous amount of unnecessary pain and suffering.

Decision-making has become very difficult for me, even almost two years later. I would prefer that someone else make choices. I believe this is because I had to take charge, both during my husband's heart attack recovery and for my father's caregiving. A psychological reaction to those experiences has been the inability to make up my mind and stick to it. Those supporting the caregiver need to understand the caregiver's needs in this area, particularly after caregiving is over.

Caregivers often don't see themselves and what is happening to them. They don't realize the stresses they are enduring by coping under pressure, reacting to unexpected occurrences and handling major life-and-death crises. There is nothing that prepares them to handle all of the emotional and physical encounters that lie ahead. They don't fully realize what is going on in their own bodies — the physical, emotional, psychological, social, and spiritual realigning they are experiencing.

Physical

As I write this chapter, I am taking yet another course of antibiotics for an upper-respiratory infection — the third in the one-and-one-half years since my father died. In addition, I've taken two courses for an infection, two courses for a staph infection, and several for other infections in the same amount of time. Undoubtedly, some of these can be blamed on a "run-down" system caused by physical stress! It's been tough, but it is seemingly normal for many caregivers. What could I have done differently to ward off some of the physical and emotional wear and tear on my body?

For one thing, I should have religiously maintained the mild physical exercise program I was on — or at least have gone for a short walk each day. Even a fifteen-minute walk in the neighborhood would have been good for mind and soul, as well as the body. Another major help would have been to plan for at least three nights of uninterrupted sleep each week. That rest alone would have helped keep up my strength. These are but two solutions, but very important ones. From the data we find that physical exercise and sleep are critical to physical and holistic well-being. According to Marilyn Ditty, a gerontology specialist. "Caregivers suffer from poor health and chronic flare-ups of illness, because they have very little resistance to infections. Their bodies have limited warranties, and they're more likely to have a constant fatigue syndrome which is the result of caring for everyone. Until the load is lifted by sharing the responsibilities of caregiving with others and asking others for help, the solitary caregiver can look forward to continual health problems — both mental and physical — which can result in the reversal of roles where the giver of care eventually becomes the taker of care."[7]

Not only should caregivers take care to have at least minimal exercise and sleep, but diet is also important, even though eating is often the last thing on your mind. In some cases, the caregiver tends not to eat well-balanced meals. You either grab a bite at the hospital cafeteria or in the patient waiting room, or you pick up fast food. And your time is very limited to do any thinking about your own meals. So you end up not only eating the things that are bad for you, but you might also overeat, depending on how you handle stress. (I added about fifteen pounds during my caregiving days.) When there is not enough time, energy, or dollars to spend on food and caring for yourself, the caregiver and family are deprived.

The Professionals Need to Take Care of Themselves Too

People involved in care management, as with the primary caregivers who live in the home, realize that there are times when they feel overwhelmed and feel like quitting.

"Whenever I feel that way, I realize it's a cue that I'm not paying enough attention to my own health and well-being. I'm here for the haul, but to do that I first need to take care of myself," says Evelyn Daws.[8]

Other professionals feel the same way. Harriett Dennison, a registered nurse, says, "You need to maintain a sense of balance between caring for others and caring for yourself. Most relationships in life are give-and-take. But when you're caring for a patient you know is dying, you tend to give more and to not expect very much in return." Dennison also says, "No matter how conscious [the caregiver] is about setting limits and tending to [personal] physical and spiritual needs, there are times when the only way to regain [his or] her sense of balance is to take some time away from caring for terminally ill patients. You can't keep giving and giving without pulling back every now and then and taking time out to rejuvenate and recapture your energy. You have to make a conscious choice to take care of yourself. If you don't you end up having nothing left to give."[9]

Dr. Ditty, Director of the San Clemente, California, Adult Day-Care Center, also said, "Illness is inevitable with chronic fatigue and depression."

Avoid Burnout

Caregivers need to be aware that they can totally burn out from caregiving. In the case of one husband, he was so overworked and stressed that he had a stroke. And, in some situations, the spouse dies before the patient.

What can the caregiver do to avoid burnout? Avoid the following, which all lead to discouragement and eventual burnout: resentment at having to give care, at always attending to another's needs; exhaustion from the never-ending tasks; sadness that the role your elder used to play in your life has changed; frustration that you don't have time for your own needs and pleasures; guilt that you wish for more gratitude than you get; anger that others don't offer more help; and exasperation at the social service system, which is difficult to pin down. All of these factors lead to stress. Feeling irritable, worried, pessimistic, preoccupied, having trouble sleeping, having physical symptoms such as diarrhea or constipation, or being unpleasant to people you care about can be signs of stress.

What should you do? Get adequate rest and nutrition; exercise regularly; get away and relax; allow others to help; talk about your frustrations; and set goals that you can achieve.[10]

Diet and exercise are extremely important. Since even a small amount of exercise improves the general health of those in nursing homes, certainly a little bit of exercise will help the caregiver. "No matter how you feel today, you don't know what may happen down the line," says Arnold Schwarzenegger, Director of the President's Council on Physical Fitness. "Exercise serves as preventive medicine. You don't have to do anything drastic. Take the stairs instead of riding the escalator. Take them two steps at a time instead of one. Walk more, swim more, exercise more."[11] It's been said that exercise is more important than having an annual physical. It certainly can do wonders for the total being, and it will help rejuvenate you, the caregiver.

There are six traits that signal to a caregiver the potential for overdoing it. If you possess three, you are a prime candidate for caregiver burnout: "Possess strong maternal instinct that compels caring for others; Strong nesting characteristic, fussing about the home, taking great pride in how it's decorated; Family ranking as the eldest, the leader or decision maker; Helping personality or a career in a helping profession such as social worker, clergy or counselor; Strong religious background, a belief that caring is ethically and morally correct; Traditional attitudes, a belief that values of the past are meaningful."[12]

There are no easy solutions when it comes to taking care of oneself, only warnings and shared experiences of other caregivers and the health care professionals.

CHAPTER TEN
The Stages of Caregiving

The experience of caregiving is like none other in a person's life. For most, it is not something to which they have even given much thought. They are unprepared for caregiving because they don't think it could ever happen to them. But it does. And most of us are surprised at ourselves and our reactions as we live through the situation.

Caregivers go through what I call the "stages of caregiving," the different feelings and emotions that are experienced. The caregiver often has difficulty dealing with some of these feelings because they are so foreign to the way that person acts normally. A calm and patient personality can become sharp and negative, and emotionally on edge. A very sociable, people-oriented person may become withdrawn, even to the point of avoiding any contact with others. Looking at these stages may be helpful to confirm that nothing is wrong with the caregiver, and that the behaviors are normal responses to the situation and can be dealt with in a positive way. Of course, it is difficult to separate all of the feelings into neat categories, because we have some or all of them at times throughout the total experience. But knowing one has normal responses at certain times over the course of the caregiving does give some relief. And facing these feelings can be a freeing experience for the caregiver. Although these stages focus primarily on the dying, they also apply to caregivers.

Stage One: Unrealistic Hopes

At the very beginning, hopes are high for care and recovery. In this stage the caregiver feels, "I can help him or her to face this." The high degree of devotion to the patient is all-consuming, and the caregiver sacrifices personal discretionary time. There is also a high level of physical energy expended, since the caregiving is just beginning. The caregiver is learning many new things about the medical and physical needs of the patient, is learning about the resources available, and is motivated to carry through with giving the patient the care needed over the long haul.

The caregiving is made up of many productive days, and each situation is a new, challenging experience for both patient and caregiver. Above all, there is the feeling that what the caregiver does will help the patient, either toward recovery or toward a palliative existence.

At this stage there is still a lot of extra help, support, interest, and encouragement being received, both for the patient and the caregiver. Those on the outside looking in are settling things with the patient. Most, however, will quickly move on with their lives. The caregiver needs and appreciates the expressions of love and concern, and experiences a sense of being cared for by friends and family.

While the caregiver is energetic and motivated, he or she is beginning to face reality, straddling the fence between, "I know this is happening, but maybe it can be fixed." There is denial that this is even happening. Denial is the defense that one uses to escape the reality of the situation: denial that a loved one is dying, that either the aging process or a dread disease or medical problem is taking place.

Stage Two: Realism

Probably this is the longest stage of caregiving. It can be reached quickly, if the caregiver is able to face some of the questions and personal problems, and to deal with them in a healthy way. There is a realistic view of the situation, an understanding that—barring a miracle—the patient is dying and/or will need long-term care.

The situation with the patient has reached the point where frequent trips to the doctors and hospital, including the use of an ambulance are becoming necessary. In fact, they are now ordinary, rather than unusual, occurrences. The illness is becoming more and more prominent in daily life. The patient's body is so weak that there are no resources to draw upon to regain the strength of even a few weeks past. Complications arise almost weekly, if not daily. The patient declines physically very quickly, but probably not mentally (with the exception of Alzheimer's).

During this stage the caregiver feels more and more helpless and hopeless, but still needs to employ a high level of resourcefulness, energy, optimism, and devotion to care. The caregiver must continue to show commitment to the patient. The patient should not feel abandoned and useless as he or she experiences the decline of the body. The dignity and worth of the individual is very important, and the caregiver still attends to that need.

The caregiver has begun the grieving process. At the same time, he or she is handling emotions that need to be faced in order to care for the dying person in a healthy and loving manner. It may seem a contradiction in terms, since denial is definitely part of the first stage of caregiving. But denial continues. Oftentimes the aging caregiver has denied his or her own aging and finds it hard to realize that the parent or relative is getting old. In the case of one's parents, there is also the realization that the emotional and psychological shelter that long has been received is no longer available, and this fact can throw life out of balance.

The denial of the situation may be accompanied by a great deal of anger that does not make sense to the caregiver. The need to lash out at someone or something surprises and often is a result of avoiding the truth of the situation.

Bob Vander Zaag, who with his wife Glenda, cared for their young child who contracted polio, said, "The parents go through stages of personal need, including that of expressing their anger toward the situation, and even toward God. Freely express anger to someone. God can handle it quite well, even though there may be those who will scold you for your inadequate faith. The parent who pretends not to have moments of anger is doing very dangerous faking, because anger comes and goes, and it always will. Hindsight tells me that family therapy would be extremely helpful, particularly if the counselor empathizes with another believer's honest doubts. Pastoral counsel that defends irrelevant theological positions often is unnecessary."

There is also the fear of the unknown. The caregiver may think, *Will I be able to handle everything I must face? I don't know enough about taking care of someone's physical needs. How can I ever manage the long days and sleepless nights? I'll be a physical wreck myself, and I won't be able to meet the demands.*

The caregiver must learn to let go—to separate from the dying while continuing to love and support. This is a complex and painful experience, even under the best of circumstances. The adult child may be angry at the parent for getting old. When the parent makes demands, the adult child feels guilty for not being able to meet those demands, and feelings of self-worth may suffer. The adult child needs to be aware that the parent is probably going through the grieving process too. He or she must be patient, rather than trying to continually please and fix things for the parent. In fact, the adult child may never be able to please the parent, and that's all right. One cannot live another's life. It's best to come to a point of resolve for yourself, and then trust that God will help your parent or aging relative do so in his or her own time and way.

Caregivers sometimes have an overwhelming feeling of guilt because they may have feelings of wanting to get away from caregiving. Closely related to this guilt feeling is the fact that the caregivers sincerely believe no one else is able to care for the parent as well as a family member, usually themselves. Some fail to seek assistance because they just do not know what help is available or how to go about finding that help.

"It was really hard not to feel guilty for having put mother in a home," Doris Stephens says, recalling the pain. "She had told me she never wanted to go to that place, but I really had no choice. I hoped that she didn't know where she was."

"Oftentimes one cannot let go of another person if there is something in the relationship that needs to be settled, to be forgiven. The adult child may have had some great difficulties with the parent, such as emotional or physical abuse, feelings of neglect because of a divorce, alcoholic problems, or other lifestyle issues that have never been faced and resolved. The caregiver is in a situation that demands a forgiveness without which the barriers will continue to grow and the demands become more difficult. The patient may never come to the point of asking forgiveness, and the caregiver must realize this. However, the caregiver is only responsible for his or her own life. The release of these feelings to God will bring healing.

"Forgiving our parents [or spouse or other relative] for being less than perfect often becomes more, not less, difficult as they age. In old age, people become what they have always been, only more so. If we have never learned to accept our parents' shortcomings and failures—whether it be a quick temper, negativism, a hostility to spiritual things, a judgmental attitude, a lack of interest in grand-children—then the accentuation of these traits in old age will surely drive us crazy," says Barbara Deane, cofounder of Christian Caregivers. Deane adds, "Responding with demands that our parents change is a self-defeating strategy that will only drive us deeper into anger and depression. It will also distract us from facing our own unforgiving and judgmental attitudes. Whether or not our parent changes, we must—for our own good."[1]

Another problem that the caregiver begins to face during this stage is that of isolation. It happens almost imperceptibly—being with other people is not a high priority while caregiving has become number one. Unless the caregiver has made a conscious effort to maintain some semblance of normalcy in schedule and being with others, even in church attendance, the shift is so subtle that it occurs unnoticed.

Sometimes the feeling of being a martyr accompanies isolation. Often, caregivers do not know that they are playing the martyr, or that they want others to feel sorry for them. There may be a need for the acknowledgment from others, including the patient, that the caregiver is hurting. Somehow, the caregiver gains some self-gratification and sense of accomplishment when this need is filled.

During this stage it is important for the caregiver to give up unrealistic expectations of his or her parents. If the adult child needs to have his or her parents be a certain way in order to make them happy, all of his or her energy will be poured into the hopeless task of trying to control the parents' illness and aging. Whenever adult children insist that this is the way a parent has to be, they're actually trying to play God.

You the caregiver may be unaware of how to go about facing the emotional problems. If this is the case, it would be wise to find a support group, a psychologist, or other counselor that can help you sort through some of the difficulties particular to your situation.

One event that may give some perspective happened during this stage in my caregiving. It is an example of realism and having to face the patient's mortality. On Christmas night my father experienced great difficulty breathing, and nothing seemed to give relief. The surgeon, who had performed my father's gall bladder surgery the month before, had made a home visit to see him on Christmas Eve. We wanted to be certain that there were no complications that would warrant bothering him during the holidays. We felt confident that my father was in no immediate danger of major distress. Thus, when he began having extraordinary difficulty breathing, we were concerned, but not alarmed. I did not want my father to suffer. I also did not want to pray that God would take him. And yet I knew God's timing was right. My father had said, "Why should I be any different from others who have to suffer through such great difficulties?" Since I did not know what to do, I went ahead with my normal way of handling his care.

First, of course, I called the doctor. The situation didn't seem to be life-threatening at that point. I was not able to reach the primary doctor on Christmas. Thus I had to communicate a lot of data about my father's case to the on-call physician. He didn't express great concern, since the surgeon had checked my father only the day before. But the situation became worse, so we tried a vaporizer. Soon in desperation, I called for emergency oxygen from the home-care respiratory supplier. Then my father became dramatically worse within a very short time. In retrospect, I think he may have had a heart attack; he simply could not breathe well. The oxygen did not help, and his blood pressure nearly bottomed out.

Of course, the caregiver has no time to stop and discuss things. One has only time to cry out inside, "God, help me know what to do!" Should I call 911? Or is this the time when I let him go? My decision was based on this thinking: My father's cancer was not fast-growing, but he was dying—that was for certain. He had had the gall bladder surgery, which was extremely hard for him on top of the cancer. The weakened condition of his body could be causing him some difficulty, but if taken care of, he could live a few months longer. And because he was bright, alert, and intellectually and emotionally a part of ongoing life, I did not think that this was the time to let him go, particularly if his obvious suffering of the hour was something that could be cared for. Besides, he seemed to want to take care of the problem.

So I called 911. Because of his situation, they told me to

call an ambulance. Within fifteen minutes he was in the emergency room and admitted to a hospital room. Doctors discussed his problem, which, in fact, was caused by his gall bladder surgery. (The drainage tube—T-tube—placed in his abdomen following the surgery had been removed before the area had healed, and his system was filled with poisons from the drainage.) The doctors immediately scheduled him for surgery to repair the area the next day.

The surgery could have taken his life, but it could also give him some more time. If he did nothing, he would die within a few days. My sisters were summoned, and they had a few hours with Daddy before the operation. They also spent some time with him following the surgery. These visits were precious both to them and Daddy. Again, the realism of the situation set in—he was dying, and we had to deal with that fact.

When my father chose the surgery, it was the first time that we all felt direct, strategic communication that said, "This may be it. Death may be at hand." We had talked about death and dying; we had prepared for it. But now, it actually could be here. Even in my father's weakened condition, however, knowing that he could die in surgery, we still clung to hope.

The surgery gave him another month of life, during which time he was able to witness to several about his faith, leading at least one person to a knowledge of Christ as Savior. He was able to tie up the loose ends of his life in such a way that, when the time came, he knew it was time to die. And so did I.

Stage Three: Maintenance

During this stage the caregiver and the patient both know that the end is certain and near, although the timing of death is unknown. The caregiver's energy level is almost depleted, but one must continue on because of the commitment and the devotion to the patient. It's not that the caregiver wants to stop the caregiving. It's just that personal resources are very thin. During this time, as one begins to feel drained, inefficient, and helpless, it is important to keep guilt from creeping into your thoughts in reaction to your personal feelings.

I still have guilt to deal with for one situation. I felt strongly that I needed to get out of the house and attend a special church service. I was determined to go, fixing things for my father so he could manage for the short time I would be gone. I will never forget the look on his face the following morning when he gently said, "I'm a real bother to you." This was one of the most difficult things for me to hear, because that was simply not the case. But by insisting I attend this service, in the bustle of getting ready to leave him I had made him feel like he was a burden. Over the course of the next few weeks I tried to let him know that he certainly was not a bother, but a joy to have around. The guilt that I took upon myself was unwarranted, but it is an example of what a caregiver can do without thinking, both to himself or herself and to the patient during this stage of caring.

At this stage resources are waning, and there is a sense that some of the medical professionals are pulling back from the emotional support that is so necessary at the end of life. Thankfully, my father's primary doctors never gave this impression to either my father or me. But when one of the specialists was called in to advise on a particular problem, he used words that cut through to my inner being: "Carol, he's dying anyway."

The harsh reality of that statement made me realize that many people had viewed my father as dying, while, until this stage, I had been functioning on hope. I do not fault the doctor. Doctors see death on a regular basis, and they must give care without getting too emotionally involved with a patient. But I realized from his statement that death was expected and the time was getting close.

I was trying to maintain the best quality of life that was possible for my father, while others were already standing by expecting the end.

Balance for the caregiver during this stage of caregiving is absolutely essential. One must recognize the inevitability of death, while enjoying the remainder of life. Life, until the moment of death, must be meaningful and worthwhile. Each human being is a God-created person of worth until his or her final breath. The last thing my father said to me was a word of encouragement for our son, following their last prayer together. I was amazed — as he was dying, he was still ministering to us.

Through this most difficult stage, the caregiver should not give up. He or she must trust that God Himself will sustain and uplift, as the inevitable — death — approaches. And by all means, make the effort to enjoy the last special, precious minutes of life.

CHAPTER ELEVEN
Spiritual Nourishment for the Caregiver

The spiritual aspects of the caregiver's life are of primary concern now more than ever. One must be focused and grounded in faith, trusting in the hope of the Christian and strengthened by the Holy Spirit. Hope is primary for the caregiver, as well as for the patient. My husband, John, said of hope, "I would pray each night with Dad, focusing on the peace of God and the hope that comes from the work of the Holy Spirit in our lives. I prayed he would find that the Holy Spirit would minister through his suffering and would help continue to build in him a character full of hope—hope and comfort in the present disease, a peace of knowing God's presence with him, and a renewed hope in the present illness. I'd pray with thanks for the future, whatever the outcome might be for his disease."

The most important thing a caregiver can do is to reassure the patient of the hope that is his or hers through salvation. Ron Shackelford said, "The caregiver should be certain that the patient has the assurance of salvation; the patient may need to affirm a personal faith and trust in the relationship with Jesus Christ and the knowledge that he or she will be in heaven." If the patient is not certain of this, the caregiver must take the opportunity to talk with the patient about the hope the believer enjoys because of

Christ's death and resurrection for our sins.

> Because of His great love for us, God, who is rich in
> mercy, made us alive with Christ even when we were
> dead in transgressions — it is by grace you have been
> saved. And God raised us up with Christ and seated
> us with Him in the heavenly realms in Christ Jesus, in
> order that in the coming ages He might show the
> incomparable riches of His grace, expressed in His
> kindness to us in Christ Jesus.
>
> For it is by grace you have been saved, through
> faith . . . not by works, so that no one can boast (Eph.
> 2:4-9).

It seems that the caregiver depends on God's daily guidance and sustenance now, more than at any other time in
life. God gives courage, physical energy, strength, and joy
in caring for another, and the Holy Spirit brings comfort
when all is despair. I certainly found this to be true.

Research is confirming that one's faith affects caregiving.
The spiritual dimension of one's life — the relationship
with Jesus Christ and a new understanding of servanthood
for the Christian — is the basis for the quality of care for
many people. In fact, personal spirituality encourages
someone to care for other people. Recent research has
found this to be the case. "In an effort to determine why
some people are exceptionally caring, psychologists,
studying members of religious orders, found that the quality separating members who find joy in caring for the
poorest of the poor, from those who respond out of duty,
is the depth of their personal relationship with God."[1]
These are the findings of David McClelland, professor
emeritus of psychology at Harvard University, and Carol
Franz of Boston University. Their research is part of a larger study funded by the Lilly Endowment, entitled, "The
Future of Religious Orders in the U.S." The study divided
the target audience, members of religious orders, into two
groups, those who were "exceptionally caring," and those

who were identified by their communities as "typical ... but who still would be considered as helpful and caring."[2]

McClelland and Franz found that people "help others out of self-interest—either to fulfill a personal desire to aid others or to reduce the guilt felt for walking by someone in need." Another reason for caring was stated to be because of "a benevolent authority ... more simply, God."[3] The people in the "exceptionally caring" group had more joy in their work, "were more likely to establish personal relationships with the people they helped, and more likely to describe activities, such as visiting the sick and helping the poor, as being very valuable."[4] When the participants in this study were asked to describe an experience of healing, "four times as many in the caring religious group mentioned God's role in the experience." Contemplative prayer was frequently described as being very valuable by this caring group. Those who were deemed as "exceptional carers" had more joy and felt that their caregiving was a valuable experience.

The researchers concluded that "relying upon God produced some practical benefits" for caregivers, such as avoiding burnout. Because of the reliance on God for healing, caregivers are "less likely to be manipulative ... because they believe it is God, not they, that is the source of the healing." Caregivers see themselves as "coming from and identified with something larger than themselves," McClelland says. "Sharing their relationship with God is more important than fixing the immediate need of the individual." Spiritual caregivers "don't stress the suffering and need ... nearly as much as those who have socialized power motives. Take Mother Teresa as an example. The reason she can describe the joy in picking worms off a homeless man who will die a few hours later is 'because this is the way she identifies with Jesus and the way He would want it.' "[5]

The researchers in this study discovered what many Christians have known and experienced through the ages:

the *joy of giving care to others* is inexpressible and comes from one's relationship with the ultimate caregiver, God the Father, through the power of the Holy Spirit. Although burnout, physical problems, stresses, and sometimes over- whelming problems may arise, the Christian has unbeliev- able resources that come from God, that empower and give strength and courage in the darkest hours. And that's why this chapter is very important to this book.

How does one draw upon those resources, the inner strength, the courage, and hope that reside in the believ- er? It is human to feel hopeless and helpless, and to even withdraw from the organized opportunities that we have for growth, such as church services. Bob Vander Zaag said of their early years caring for their young daughter: "Spiri- tually there were times when we were so drained that if we did not have to be at church on Sundays, we might have lapsed into a very lax attitude toward church atten- dance and maintaining of any spiritual discipline whatever. However, none of the emotions that we experienced were permanent and everything undulated normally."

Our physical stamina is so fragile that the stresses of caregiving take a toll on the total being. How does the caregiver bring spiritual nourishment and physical energy into balance with each other?

The lifestyle of Christianity that the caregiver has experi- enced during the noncaregiving years is basic and, certain- ly for many, provides a foundation of trust and communi- cation with God during the lean times. I've personally experienced periods of peace, joy, blessing, and special times of energizing just before a very difficult period in life. It's as though a storing up of body, soul, and spirit occurs. I've learned (sometimes the hard way!) to enjoy and take full advantage of such times for more Scripture reading, prayer, and personal rejuvenation. These times are to be relished and enjoyed because often in the lean periods — the periods of spiritual drought — there is no op- portunity to really enjoy the contemplative, reflective mo- ments. This is particularly true for the caregiver. For most, caregiving can be a lean time with little or no freedom to focus on one's own personal spiritual needs. One must draw from the stored resources of past experiences of spiritual growth.

What if the caregiver has not spent quality time in personal devotion? God truly does care, no matter what our normal Christian walk was. He will give all that we need, if we ask. We must trust Him for the resources, for He does provide. God has promised to be with us, whether we've been in the habit of personal devotion or not.

It may seem impossible to think of stopping for a moment to read a Scripture verse. Yet I firmly believe the rich resources of Scripture will bring peace, joy, and strength. One of my father's friends made a lovely cross-stitching that sat in a frame on his dresser: "The joy of the Lord is your strength."[6] This verse was intended for my father's encouragement, but I quoted and prayed it almost each time I passed by. I didn't have time to stop and look it up in the Bible, but it sat there as a constant reminder of God's promise to me.

I selected the thoughts in the remainder of this chapter for the busy caregiver, for your personal nourishment. If you have time to read the Scriptures for yourself, that is great. If not, have someone copy them on cards and put them by your bedside or sink for a quick, on-the-run devotional time to read in passing.

Some of the following thoughts are shared from the experiences of caregivers who have walked where other caregivers are now walking. They express the deep aches of heart and soul, and the spiritual strength and love of Christ shown through caring.

Commitment and Devotion to Your Loved One

"In sickness and health . . . till death do us part." These words spoke clearly to Robertson McQuilkin (former president of Columbia Bible College and Seminary, Columbia, South Carolina), who made the choice to resign his position as president in order to devote his time to the care his wife needed at home, rather than have her placed in a nursing home. He wrote about his feelings when his wife of over forty years slowly withdrew into the dark shadows of Alzheimer's disease:

> There is that subterranean grief that will not go away. I feel just as alone as if I had never known her as she was, I suppose, but the loneliness of the night hours come because I did know her. Do I grieve for her loss or mine?
>
> This was no grim duty to which I was stoically resigned, however. It was only fair. She had, after all, cared for me for almost four decades with marvelous devotion; now it was my turn. And such a partner she was! If I took care of her for forty years, I would never be out of her debt. As I watch her brave descent into oblivion, Muriel is the joy of my life. She is such a delight to me. I don't *have* to care for her, I *get* to. Daily I discern new manifestations of the kind of person she is, the wife I always loved. I also see fresh manifestations of God's love—the God I long to love more fully.[7]

Satisfy us in the morning with your unfailing love, that we may sing for joy and be glad all our days (Ps. 90:14).

Receiving Care

"The Lord is my shepherd, I shall not be in want" (Ps. 23:1).

How many times has this Scripture passage brought comfort to the ill and dying? I quoted those words to my husband, John, as he came out of a coma after his heart attack. He relied on this psalm during his recuperation and return to normal life. Nathan Goff, a minister and Director of Church Relations at Gordon College in Massachusetts, tells of a time before surgery when he too dwelt on this well-known passage. He had already experienced three heart attacks and angioplasty, and was facing quadruple bypass surgery.

"Flat on the gurney as I rolled toward the operating room those words swept over my mind like ocean breakers. . . . The great, sovereign, majestic almighty God is my Shepherd. He is the One who treats me as a shepherd treats his sheep. He cares for me. He is concerned about me. He provides for me. He knows what is best for me. He does not guarantee escape from all trouble and difficulty. I knew I was passing into the unknown beyond those operating room doors. But I also knew I was not alone—He was with me. I had His Word, and that was my anchor. As the doors opened to the brightly lit operating room, the phrase 'God is good' came as if written on the ceiling."

God's goodness is promised to us when the Apostle Paul said, "And we know that in all things God works for the good of those who love Him, who have been called according to His purpose" (Rom. 8:28).

"One day, if not on this planet then in the life to come, we will realize that the twists and bumps, including our times as health-care receivers," continues Goff, "were part of His eternal purpose for our good to make us more like the Lord Jesus."[8] The caregiver can express these words of encouragement and hope to the patient. But they can be equally as pertinent and helpful to oneself. In all the difficult times God is working out His purpose in your life, and He is good.

Bad Things Do Happen

Life is incomprehensible. Why is there sickness and evil? Why must our loved one suffer? Where is God when we see this happening? Does He still love us? Is He punishing us?

Many of us ask these and other questions, sometimes out of anger, but more often out of despair and frustration. The "Why, God?" questions punctuate even the life of the Christian, and sometimes they are more obvious when we see the suffering and dying of a loved one, day in and day out. "Do we actually believe, deep down, that 'bad things really don't happen to good (truly Spirit-filled) people'? To admit to the reality of sickness and suffering seems to many Christians to be a denial of the deliverance the Gospel seems to promise."⁹ Theologians and philosophers have wrestled with these and other questions for years. The Book of Job talks about some of these struggles when Job argued with God. And yet, through all of his difficulties and suffering, Job experienced the power, righteousness, and comfort of God, and God blessed him for his faithfulness to Him and hope in Him. Even though he struggled and questioned, Job remained faithful and repented for his lack of confidence and belief in God's power.

God promised to be with us, even today, as He was with the Israelites:

I will never leave you or forsake you (Josh. 1:5).

Jesus said:

Lo, I am with you alway, even unto the end of the earth (Matt. 28:20, KJV).

Jesus also said one of the most comforting things:

I have told you these things, so that in Me you may have peace. In this world you will have trouble. But take heart! I have overcome the world (John 16:33, NIV).

Strength for Today ... And Tomorrow Too?

The uncertainty of death is difficult, both for the caregiver and the patient. The patient may not be able to express it, but certainly he or she is always thinking about it. What hope and encouragement can the caregiver give? How can hope be rekindled with day after day of uncertainty?

Perhaps these words give a hint at the need to live daily, pleasing God:

> Just as you received Christ Jesus as Lord, continue to live in Him, rooted and built up in Him, strengthened in the faith as you were taught, and overflowing with thankfulness (Col. 2:6).

A young mother faced a very uncertain future. She was diagnosed with cancer which had metastasized. She struggled with her emotions and the "cry of her heart, 'My God, my God, why have You forsaken Me?' " She recalls, "Finding myself at the crossroads between now and death, I faced a litany of issues. I had choices and decisions to make. Although I had not chosen the cancer, I did have a choice in terms of my response. The threatening disease was fast becoming my primary focus. It followed me through the day; it haunted me throughout the night. There was no place to hide. I could no longer carry on in my own inadequate strength. I had come to the end of myself. I came to a choice of trust and hope. God met me where I was. Restoration began. Christ became my hope."[10] The Apostle Paul said:

> Three times I pleaded with the Lord to take it away from me [the thorn in the flesh]. But He said to me, "My grace is sufficient for you, for My power is made perfect in weakness." Therefore I will boast all the more gladly about my weaknesses, so that Christ's power may rest on me. That is why, for Christ's sake, I delight in weaknesses, in insults, in hardships, in persecutions, in difficulties. For when I am weak, then I am strong (2 Cor. 12:8-10).

The young mother came to a place of peace and trust in

God's care and love, which led her to say, "You, Lord, are all I have, and You give me all I need (taken from Ps. 16). My future is in Your hands."[11]

Pray Continually . . . Even When You Can't

Charles H. Spurgeon, the great English preacher, reminds us, "Our extremities are the Lord's opportunities."[12] But how can we, in the most extreme times of frustration and discouragement, possibly see our situation as God's possibility? We simply don't understand God's ways, but we can, even in the midst of trying times, give thanks. Thanks, for what? Scripture tells us:

> Be joyful always; pray continually; give thanks in all circumstances, for this is God's will for you in Christ Jesus (1 Thes. 5:16-18).

It is very difficult to thank God for the hard times, for the way our loved one must suffer, for the terrible accident that has maimed our child for life, for the imminent death of a young person. Realistically, it doesn't make sense. It's hard to even pray. Yet Scripture tells us not only are we to be joyful, but also to pray continually:

> In the same way, the Spirit helps us in our weakness. We do not know what we ought to pray, but the Spirit Himself intercedes for us with groans that words cannot express. And He who searches our hearts knows the mind of the Spirit, because the Spirit intercedes for the saints in accordance with God's will (Rom. 8:26-27).

Many, many times I could not pray. I sat in the middle of the stairway with my head in my hands, crying out to God: "Help! I can't pray, and I don't know what to do next. How can I go another step?" I had no joy, and I was speechless with my prayers. At such times God meets us where we are. And He gives us the strength to continue and the joy to share with our loved one, who needs both. How wonderful to know we have superhuman strength and joy! I believe God wants us to communicate with Him continually, even when we're not in the middle of a trying time. And when we are in the middle, He knows what our heart is trying to say, and His Spirit says it for us.

My Loved One Is Suffering, and I Feel Helpless

One of the most difficult times of caregiving is when you see the agony and suffering of your loved one, and there's nothing you can do but watch and pray. This was true when my father experienced the congestion that comes from pneumonia and fluids in the lungs toward the end of his life. It is difficult to even write about this — it's a painful memory.

Again, I go to that old devotional book by Charles H. Spurgeon,[13] who quotes the Scripture from 1 Peter 5:7:

Cast all your anxiety on Him because He cares for you.

We Have Hope for the Future — Life after Death

The believer has the assurance and peace that God has planned our lives and that He controls life and death, and the life that is to come. It is extremely hard to imagine what it will be like. Yet because of His promises we have hope and can rest peacefully even through the suffering and trials of an imperfect world. According to 1 Peter 1:3-12, the Apostle Peter talked about hope, and how we can live through suffering. The last verses of that chapter quote from a psalm, which talks about the God who is faithful forever:

All men are like grass, and all their glory is like the flowers of the field; the grass withers and the flowers fall, but the Word of the Lord stands forever (1 Peter 1:24-25).

What Will Heaven Be Like?

The thought of heaven and being in the presence of God is incomprehensible. We cannot conceive of such an experience. Yet, as we watch a loved one die and know he or she will soon enter such a place, we try to figure out the mystery of life after death, being in a place such as Scripture describes:

> Then I saw a new heaven and a new earth, for the first heaven and the first earth had passed away, and there was no longer any sea. I saw the Holy City, the New Jerusalem, coming down out of heaven from God, prepared as a bride beautifully dressed for her husband. And I heard a loud voice from the throne saying, "Now the dwelling of God is with men, and He will live with them. They will be His people, and God Himself will be with them and be their God. He will wipe every tear from their eyes. There will be no more death or mourning or crying or pain, for the old order of things has passed away."
>
> He who was seated on the throne said, "I am making everything new!" Then He said, "Write this down, for these words are trustworthy and true."
>
> He said to me: "It is done. I am the Alpha and the Omega, the Beginning and the End. To him who is thirsty I will give to drink without cost from the spring of the water of life. He who overcomes will inherit all this, and I will be his God and he will be My son (Rev. 21:1-7).

According to 2 Corinthians 5:8, the Apostle Paul talked about our heavenly home, when he said it is preferable "to be away from the body and at home with the Lord." Or as *The Living Bible* says, "We are not afraid, but are quite content to die, for then we will be at home with the Lord."

Another Scripture on heaven is Isaiah 64:17-18:

Behold, I will create new heavens and a new earth. The former things will not be remembered, nor will they come to mind. But be glad and rejoice forever in what I will create, for I will create Jerusalem to be a delight and its people a joy.

The rest of this passage talks more about what heaven will be like (vv. 19-25). The joy of the Christian—to be in the presence of a great God—is overwhelming when you stop and think about it. It certainly is a hope that the Christian can enjoy, even through human suffering and pain.
Hope and strength and joy, all seem interconnected.

Those who hope [put their trust] in the Lord will renew their strength. They will soar on wings like eagles; they will run and not grow weary, they will walk and not be faint (Isa. 40:31).

What a great verse for the caregiver. How thankful we can be for the great hope we have! How comforting it is to know that our lives are in the hands of the Giver of hope!

Practice Praising God All the Time

What? How can I possibly praise God when I feel as if I'm in a chasm of despair? For what can I praise God? Life is seemingly falling apart, and so am I. Several years ago a dear friend and prayer partner gave me what has become one of my favorite books, *The Hallelujah Factor*, by Jack R. Taylor. This book is crammed full of Scripture and experiences based on the most important thing in life—praising God. Even as I write these words, I am again reminded of the power and strength that comes through during the most difficult days. I would go to the piano and play a hymn or a praise song, or listen to a tape. The buoying up of praise and adoration to God gives the believer that hope and sustenance. Taylor says, "No exercise will result in more healing physically, mentally, emotionally, and spiritually than that of studying and practicing praise."[14]

When one is beyond the point of expressing anything at all, praise the Lord. When your loved one has taken a turn for the worse, praise the Lord. How can this be?

Remember the story of Jehoshaphat in 2 Chronicles 20? Taylor used this chapter as an example of praising God when things are falling apart, because God is to be praised no matter what. "Everything was simply in a mess," he says. Jehoshaphat remembered that the Lord had cared for His people in the past, and he believed in Him. "If calamity comes upon us . . . you will hear and save us," Jehoshaphat told God. "We do not know what to do." How many times does the anxious caregiver say this, feeling totally weak and unable to go on? "But our eyes are upon You," Jehoshaphat said.[15] When we look at our situation, we feel so inadequate. But Taylor continues: "If we look at our problems or our own weaknesses we shall soon despair. Not so with preoccupation with God. This is the heart of praise—our eyes are on You, our God's not problem-centered. Neither is praise human-centered. Praise is God-centered!"[16] Scripture confirms the truth that God is with us: "Do not be afraid or discouraged because of this vast army [or this caregiving dilemma]. For the battle is not yours, but God's."[17] The cry of the people as they obeyed God was, "Give thanks to the Lord, for His love endures forever!"[18]

I love what Taylor says at the end of his book: "Praise does more than enable us to survive. It enables us to thrive." Although we may not understand, the practice of praise brings joy and strength and the hope that causes both the caregiver and the believing patient to know God's richness and enabling power that He gives to the weakest. "Praise the Lord; for His mercy endureth forever.[19]

Scriptures of Praise

I will praise the Lord, who counsels me; even at night my heart instructs me. I have set the Lord always before me. Because He is at my right hand, I will not be shaken. Therefore my heart is glad and my tongue rejoices; my body also will rest secure (Ps. 16:7-9).

You have made known to me the path of life; You will fill me with joy in Your presence, with eternal pleasures at Your right hand (Ps. 16:11).

I love You, O Lord, my strength. The Lord is my rock . . . in whom I take refuge. He is my shield and the horn of my salvation, my stronghold (Ps. 18:1-2).

The Lord is my light and my salvation—whom shall I fear? The Lord is the stronghold of my life—of whom shall I be afraid? (Ps. 27:1)

Praise be to the Lord for He has heard my cry for mercy. The Lord is my strength and my shield; my heart trusts in Him and I am helped. My heart leaps for joy and I will give thanks to Him in song. The Lord is the strength of His people, a fortress of salvation for His anointed one (Ps. 28:6-8).

Let everything that has breath praise the Lord. Praise the Lord (Ps. 150:6).

Yet I will rejoice in the Lord, I will be joyful in God my Savior. The Sovereign Lord is my strength; He makes my feet like the feet of a deer (Hab. 3:18-19).

Rejoice in the Lord always. I will say it again: Rejoice! Let your gentleness be evident to all. The Lord is near (Phil. 4:4-5).

Amen! Praise and glory and wisdom and thanks and honor and power and strength be to our God forever and ever. Amen! (Rev. 7:12)

Then I heard what sounded like a great multitude, like the roar of rushing waters and like loud peals of thunder, shouting: "Hallelujah! For our Lord God Almighty reigns. Let us rejoice and be glad and give Him the glory! For the wedding of the Lamb has come, and His bride has made herself ready (Rev. 19:6-7).

Praise and thank God for His goodness and care, no matter what the circumstances. And may His rich blessings and comfort and peace pick you up and carry you when you cannot walk another step. He will be faithful to do just that and give you what you need, just as you need. To Him be glory and praise!

Appendix A
"Grandfather"

Beth Ann Dettoni:

I loved my grandfather. I didn't realize how much, though, until he came to live with us during the last months of life. I got to know him during that time in an entirely new way. I was allowed the rare experience of caring for him with the kind of love that he had shown me all my life. There is something about the fact of facing death together that cuts through all of the extraneous matters of living and permits people to interact on a deeper level. I won't pretend that it was easy adding an eighty-three-year-old man to a household of four adults, but the effort was worth it. Those nine-and-a-half months were among the best in my life. I consider them a gift from God.

It may sound strange to call my participation in the dying process a "gift," but I know that my brother and cousins would agree with me. What a privilege to see our grandfather model what it is to die in the hope of Christ, to witness a man who had faithfully served God throughout his life and know that the faith he had preached was true. We saw him in the worst times, facing the ultimate fear of every human, yet he remained strong. He was not without fear; he struggled with his illness and asked God, "Why?" But in his last months, I saw in him the peace that passes understanding.

At one point, I asked Grandfather what he had learned through the pain and suffering. He said, "Well, after living as much as I could for the Lord, to have to end this way . . . I have asked God, 'Why do You not answer my prayer and take me home, or give me the quality of life that the doctors were hoping for me?' I was hoping to be well. I asked Him, 'Why? Why didn't You heal me?' " Then Grandfather said, "The answer is 'BECAUSE.' This experience is for the glory of the Lord."

I don't know how to capture into words what it was like to care for my grandfather; I can only describe what took place in those months. For me, the initial impact of Grandfather's cancer was colored by my mother's reaction. We had been through my father's heart attack together, and that was certainly difficult. But he was out of grave danger fairly quickly. I saw a completely different dynamic concerning my grandfather; he was her *father*, and suddenly she was the child experiencing what every child dreads — the loss of a parent. And I too felt a child again, watching my parent broken and helpless to fix it.

Once Grandfather arrived at our house, however, everyone pulled together and got down to the business of taking care of him and, even more, of being there for him. I was shocked at his appearance when he got off the plane. The chemotherapy had turned his silvery-grey hair to a fine white, and there was much less of it. His pants hung loosely, and his iron grip was lost. I wondered what was ahead of us.

We certainly changed our lifestyles. Every day at least started and ended by visiting with Grandfather, and on the days when I was home there was quite a bit more time in between — making him milkshakes, regaling him with stories about my new dog's progress in obedience school, cajoling him into eating just a little bit more, watching "Jeopardy" or yet another episode of "National Geographic," discussing my future, etc. As the months went on and he underwent surgery, then began to deteriorate steadily, his care needs became more personal. I sat by him in the hospital room and put chapstick on his lips, dried his brow, wet his mouth with lollipop sponges. At home, I manicured his fingernails, fed him with a feeding tube, pulled him up out of his chair and helped him to the bathroom, and emptied the bag in which his bile was collected.

Some of these things with which I aided my Grandfather were fairly intimate, and when I first began doing them it was not easy. But they had to be done, and we both knew it. So we made the best of it, enjoying our time together with all our strength. I remember one rare night when my parents and brother were gone, and Grandfather was recently home from the hospital. After helping him to the bathroom, we tried to get him into bed correctly. He had to situate himself just right before sitting on the edge of the bed, and then I would lift his feet up while he lay down. This night he somehow ended up too far down in the bed, and he thought maybe we'd have to start all over again. But I'd been watching how the nurses were able to pull him up and thought I could manage it myself. He found the idea very amusing, though I know he was tired. "You sure you can do this?" he croaked (with a smile). And when it worked, he beamed with pleasure, said, "You did it!" and closed his eyes.

Moments like those are priceless. And I will hold them close to me for the rest of my life, for I've realized that no one will ever love me in the way my grandfather did. That bond between a grandparent and a grandchild is unique. I could make him laugh — or at least force a smile — any time I tried, just because I'm me. And he was proud of even my most minor accomplishments.

As a patient, Grandfather was ideal. He didn't complain once that I can recall. His entire focus seemed to be on God and on his family and friends, rather than on his illness and his future. One afternoon during his last hospital stay, I asked him what he was thinking about. He had a peaceful smile on his face and said, "I'm lining up people to love." My mother had a similar experience during one of his lowest times in that last week. She was with him in the hospital room when he opened his eyes with a strange look. "What are you doing, Daddy?' she asked. "I'm loving you," he said, pausing a moment and then going on, "What a life! What a joy! What a privilege!"

I have to admit that as much as I loved Grandfather, sometimes the responsibility of always being there for him was weighty. I didn't always *feel* like giving a report of my day. But I knew that, except for phone calls and visits from others, my family had become his eyes and ears to the world. In many ways, we *were* his world. He needed each one of us, and I wanted to respond to that need. Little did I know as we were going through that time that I was really the one who was growing and learning—and benefiting the most. I experienced the death process through my grandfather. I saw a faithful servant in the hours when he came face to face with his God, and how God cares for his own in the toughest times.

Perhaps because I was a part of his daily care, I knew that the timing of Grandfather's death was just right. How could I not? During his illness he constantly quoted Psalm 31:15, "My times are in His hands." He died at home, but the previous days had been spent in the hospital, where for a time he seemed very close to death. I was with him for quite a few hours then, and I believe that everyone who came into contact with him sensed that something unusual was happening.

He shone so brightly and with such love—he almost literally glowed—that it could only have come from the presence of the Holy Spirit, from Christ in him. And from his hospital bed, only three days before his death, he was busy leading a student nurse to the point of commitment to Christ.

If I manage to become even a fraction of the person that my grandfather was, making a difference in the world by serving God, I know that his example will be one of the reasons. And every single one of his grandchildren would echo that statement. At Grandfather's funeral, each one of us had the opportunity to read Scripture and say a few words. The effect that he has had on our lives was apparent. Following are his final admonitions to us, and then some of the other grandchildren's memories and reactions to Grandfather's illness:

> Tell them the Lord's admonition: Love the Lord your God with all our heart, mind and strength, and your neighbor as yourself.

Trust in the Lord with all thine heart, in all thy ways acknowledge Him—His desires . . . His wishes . . . His plans—and He shall direct thy path (Proverbs 3:5-6).

Jane Sawyer:

When I flew to Florida to take care of my grandfather, I found the man I loved dearly, just a little skinnier and more on edge than usual. He had just been diagnosed with cancer, so physically his appearance was pretty much the same.

Grandfather loved words; I think he owned the largest dictionary in print! I was in graduate school at the time and had a paper to write, so during his up times we talked and wrote. In his down times I learned to be silent but nearby.

He never really seemed to be critically ill until the day that his doctor, a family friend, stopped by. I had never seen my grandfather cry and it devastated me. To me, he was a rock who was a living testimony of God's Word. He wasn't supposed to cry. Yet he was human—he wanted to live to see his grandchildren grow up and get married. He wanted to go fishing. These were some of the desires of his heart, and his doctor/friend listened and encouraged him while I sat there with tears streaming down my cheeks. I can't tell you what I thought at that moment regarding his care and prognosis. I just sat there gaining an even deeper respect for my grandfather who had been my rock despite his pain and daily struggles.

After that night, we played along with "Jeopardy" and "Wheel of Fortune" (at least two times a day), and joked about his hair that was beginning to fall out. We tried different massage techniques and remedies to keep it in!

Nathan Hull:

When Grandfather visted us in Washington, he seemed like a different person. When he talked, it was

Grandfather, but he looked so frail and weak when he sat in his chair. It was obvious he was very tired and hurting inside.

When I first found out he had cancer I was worried, but I didn't know it could be so destructive. With all the other people I had known with cancer, they had recovered, so I had no idea what a tremendous disease cancer was. The chemotherapy seemed like something evil, and it took me awhile to tell myself that it was supposed to help him.

Carolyn Sawyer:

When Grandfather was sick, my emotions went on a roller coaster. I was mad because every time I saw him he looked more sick than the last time. That made me angry, because this was *my grandfather.* He wasn't allowed to get sick, because I didn't like to see him hurting—especially when I could not help him. But when I took care of him or just sat with him, I couldn't help but smile and laugh. He was still the same old Grandfather with the same corny jokes; they always made me smile.

Of course I missed Mom when she was gone taking care of Grandfather, but I was happy for her because she got to spend time with him and talk to him. The times when I was hurting the most were when I was at Aunt Carol's and I went and sat by myself or walked the dog down the path. That hurt because I was able to think and realize that he was dying. But it also helped me because when I was alone I realized that all the time when he was sick he stayed close to God, which brought our whole family closer to God and to each other.

After Grandfather died, that was the hardest part of all, because I had to to realize that I could not go visit him or talk to him ever again. That was the time when I hurt the most because there are so many things that you want to say to a person, but can't because they are not there anymore. What made me feel better were the memories I had of him and all the things we talked about. I also felt better because I realized the times we did have together and how much closer our family was because of that time together as a family and with God.

Ruth Hull:

Grandfather came to Yakima to visit for the last time. One of the nights he was there I had a date with my boyfriend. We had had an argument and I was really upset. It was late when I got home, and I was sitting in the living room looking out at the stars because that also helps me to relax. When Grandfather came down to get some medicine, I didn't want to startle him, so I made some noise and went over to him. He knew something was wrong but didn't ask about it. He just asked if I needed a hug. I nodded and he hugged me. Then he said, "You know who gives the best hugs?" I shook my head "no." He replied, "God gives the best hugs. And you know what? When I'm up in heaven embracing God, I'll remember to tell Him that you need one too."

Appendix B
Bibliography and Resources

Books, Booklets, and Brochures

American Association of Retired Persons (AARP) free mental health brochures, AARP Fulfillment (EE0321), P.O. Box 22796, Long Beach, Calif. 90801-5796.

Cancer Research Institute Help-Book: What to Do If Cancer Strikes, Cancer Research Institute Help-Book, FDR Station, P.O. Box 5199, New York, N.Y. 10150-5199.

The Care Giver's Mission, P.O. Box 3168, Laguna Hills, Calif. 92654-3168 ($20 includes shipping and handling).

Caregiving for Your Loved Ones, Mary Vaughan Armstrong (Elgin, Ill.: David C. Cook, 1990).

Children of Aging Parents, Woodbourne Campus Suite 302A, Dept. MM, 1609 Woodbourne Road, Levittown, Pa. 19057. For a brochure and list of materials, send SASE and $5.00.

The Christian Guide to Parent Care, Dr. Robert J. Riekse and Dr. Henry Holstege (Wheaton, Ill: Tyndale House Publishers, 1992).

The Daughter Trap, Marilyn Ditty, Ph.D. and Zondra Lewis Knapp (Smith Gibbs, 1993).

52 Ways to Show Aging Parents You Care, by Tracy Green and Todd Temple (Nashville, Tenn.: Oliver-Nelson, 1992).

Guide for Cancer Supporters, Annette and Richard Bloch, Bloch Foundation, Inc., 4410 Main Street, Kansas City, Mo. 64111. Cancer Hotline: (816) 932-8453.

"Know Your Rights before You Check into the Hospital," available from AARP, Fulfillment, P.O. Box 22796, Long Beach, Calif. 90801-5796.

Parent Care Advisor, American Health Consultants (800) 688-2421. (Charter subscriptions $39 for 12 monthly issues.)

Steps to Selecting Activities for the Person with Alzheimer's Disease: (800) 272-3900.

Aging
Administration on Aging, Department of Health and Human Services, 200 Independence Avenue, S.W., Washington, D.C. 20201.

American Geriatrics Society, 10 Columbus Circle, #1470, New York, N.Y. 10019.

The American Health Care Association, 1201 L Street NW, Washington, D.C. 20005. (202) 842-4444. Various pamphlets about long-term care facilities.

American Society on Aging (ASA), 830 Market Street, Suite 512, San Francisco, Calif. 94102. (415) 882-2910.

National Association of Area Agencies on Aging (NAAAA), 1112 16th Street NW, Suite 100, Washington, D.C. 20036. (202) 296-8130. To find the area agency on aging, call this number or the Department of Social Services. This agency will give information on the services that are available in your area.

National Council on Aging, Caregivers Program, 600 Maryland Avenue, S.W., West Wing #100, Washington, D.C. 20024. This agency will give information on long-term care, Medicaid, housing options, and long-distance caregiving, etc., (202) 479-1200.

National Support Center for Families of the Aging, P.O. Box 245, Swarthmore, Pa. 19081.

United States Eldercare Referral Agency, Inc., 14591 Newport Avenue, #202, Tustin, Calif. 92680. (800) 677-1116.

Care Management
For the American Association of Retired People (AARP) booklets, *Care Management* (D13803) and *Miles Away and Still Caring: A Guide for Long-Distance Caregivers* (D12748), send a postcard to: AARP Fulfillment (EE0307), P.O. Box 22796, Long Beach, Calif. 90801-5796. (Allow six to eight weeks for delivery.)

National Association of Geriatric Care Managers, 655 N. Alvernon, Suite 108, Tucson, Ariz. 85711 (602) 881-8008.

Care Options, 2102 Business Center Drive, Suite 130, Irvine, Calif. 92715 (714) 253-4104. This is a nonprofit organization providing education, information, guidance, and assistance to caregivers of elderly loved ones. It offers the following helps:

"Caregiving Solutions: A Beginner's Guide for Caregivers of the Elderly," an eight-sided tape series, volume 1, includes Care Planning Organizer and Resource Booklet ($39.95, plus $3.50 for postage and handling, plus tax where applicable). Tape series includes: Aging and the Sandwiched Generation; Helping with Physical Decline; Arthritis, Heart Disease, Diabetes, etc.; Coping with Mental Loss: Alzheimer's Disease and Other Dementias; Locating Community Resources: Financial, Physical, and Emotional Supports; Deciding on Alternative Living Arrangements: When and Where to Go?; Dealing with Your Feelings: Love, Guilt, and Anger; The Steps of Decision Making: Your Keys to Coping.

Also available from Care Options is an audio cassette tape program, *Caregiving Solutions: Legal Issues and Long Term Care — Avoiding a Financial Crisis.* Care Options offers a membership program with a quarterly newsletter and Information Warm-Line for an annual fee of $60.00.

Pain
Committee on Pain Therapy and Acupuncture, American Society of Anesthesiologists, 515 Busse Highway, Park Ridge, Ill. 60068.

American Pain Society, 340 Kingsland Street, Nutley, N.J. 07110.

Hospice Programs
National Hospice Organization, Suite 901, 1901 North Moore Street, Arlington, Va. 22209. (703) 243-5900.

AIDS
AIDS National Hotline: (800) 342-AIDS; (800) 344-7432 (Spanish); (800) 243-7889 (Hearing Impaired).

Alzheimer's Disease
Alzheimer's Association: (800) 272-3900.

Arthritis
Arthritis Foundation, 1314 Spring St., NW, Atlanta, Ga. 30309. (800) 283-7800.

Cancer
American Cancer Society, Inc., 777 Third Avenue, New York, N.Y. 10017. (212) 586-8700.

Cancer Information Service: 1-800-4-CANCER.

Leukemia Society of America, Inc., 733 Third Avenue, New York, N.Y. 10017. (212) 573-8484.

National Cancer Information Service: (800) 638-6694.

National Cancer Institute, Office of Cancer Communications, Building 31, Room 10A18, Bethesda, Md. 20205.

National Coalition for Cancer Survivorship, 323 Eighth Street SW, Albuquerque, N.M. 87102. (301) 650-8868.

Diabetes
American Diabetes Association: (800) 232-3472.

Eye Care
National Eye Care Project: (800) 222-EYES. A national public service project for seniors who cannot afford regular routine eye exams.

National Society to Prevent Blindness: (800) 331-2020.

Hearing Impairment
GTE Special Needs Center: (800) 821-2585 (Voice/TDD).

Hearing Aid Helpline: (800) 521-5247.

National Association for Hearing and Speech: (800) 638-8255.

Heart
American Heart Association: (214) 373-6300.

Incontinence
HIP, P.O. Box 544, Union, S.C. 29379. (800) BLADDER.

Respiratory
American Lung Association, (212) 315-8700.

Stroke
For a brochure on strokes: "Know the Warning Signs of Stroke," write 3401 Hillview Avenue, Palo Alto, Calif. 94303.

Other Resources
Consumer Credit Counseling Service. Problems paying bills: Call this nonprofit agency: (800) 388-2227.

Council on Family Health, P.O. Box 307, Coventry, Conn. 06238. "A Guide for Older Americans," on medications is available free.

Home Delivered Meals—a federally funded program available nationwide.

Home Health Express, 49 Walnut Street, Unit #4, Norwood, N.J. 07648. An at-home shopping service for medical supplies.

Meals on Wheels is a private organization, available in many parts of the country.

Medicare—Medicaid
General Services Administration, Consumer Information Center, Dept. 518Y, Pueblo, Colo. 81009. "Guide to Health Insurance for People with Medicare" is available from this organization. This provides basic information on

what seniors should know about private health insurance, and a chart explaining which services are and are not covered by Medicare.

Health Insurance Association of America, P.O. Box 41455, Washington, D.C. 20018. "The Consumer's Guide to Medicare Supplement Insurance," is a free booklet available from this organization.

National Organization of Social Security, claimants representative: (800) 431-2804. A helpful booklet is "Your Medicare Handbook," available from any Social Security office.

Legal Assistance
Legal Aid Society. Check in your local telephone directory.

National Academy of Elder Law Attorneys, Inc., Tucson, Ariz. 85711. (602) 881-4005.

Other Insurance Concerns
Health Advocacy Service, AARP, 4201 Long Beach Boulevard, #422, Long Beach, Calif. 90807. (310) 628-1161. Free insurance brochures.

National Association of Insurance Commissioners, 120 West 12th Street, #1100, Kansas City, Mo. 64105. Free booklet: "A Shopper's Guide to Long-Term Care Insurance."

National Consumers League, 815 15 Street, NW, #516, Washington, D.C. 20005. Consumer brochures to assist in understanding insurance issues.

Senior Housing
Primeline 800, 4350 Executive Drive, #310, San Diego,

Calif. 92121. (800) 433-0092. This organization provides details on all kinds of senior housing anywhere in the United States.

Nursing Homes
The American Association of Homes for the Aging, 1129 20th Street, NW, Suite 400, Washington, D.C. 20036. (202) 783-2242.

Nursing Home Information Service, 925 15th Street, NW, Washington, D.C. 20005. (202) 347-8800.

Ombudsmen Program. The long-term care through this program can be contacted through the State Department of Health and Human Services, Administration on Aging. Check your local telephone directory.

U.S. Department of Health and Human Services (Nursing Homes), 5600 Fisher Lane, Rockville, Md. 20858.

Home Nursing
Visiting Nurse Association, VNA, a national organization. Check with your local directory.

Many other privately owned home nursing companies are being formed across the country. Some of these work closely with doctor and hospital staffs, who recommend them. Check with your physician for his or her recommendation.

Health Care Ministry
Health Ministry Associates, 2427 Country Lane, Poland, Ohio 44514. (800) 852-5613. This association encompasses the church, laity, health profession, and families in the church, and assists in establishing programs on the local levels.

Parish Nurse Resource Center, Park Ridge, Ill. (708) 696-8773.

Education

Institute of Lifelong Learning, 1909 K Street NW, Washington, D.C. 20049. (800) 228-8813.

TeleCourses—for a brochure, write: Annenberg CPB Project, 1111 16th Street, NW, Washington, D.C. 20036.

Endnotes

Introduction

1. Eugenia Anderson-Ellis and Marsha Dryan, *Aging Parents & You* (New York: Master Media Limited, 1988), 10.
2. "ABC Nightly News," November 10, 1992.
3. Robert A. Rosenblatt, "Old Age Means New Problems, Report Warns," *The Los Angeles Times* (November 10, 1992), A5.
4. Alana Peters, Care Options, 2102 Business Center Drive, Suite 130, Irvine, Calif. 92715.
5. "ABC Nightly News," April 24, 1991.
6. *Time* (September 21, 1992), 18.
7. Peters.
8. Lawrence P. Ball, "Elder Care: Making It Company Policy," *Orange County Business Journal,* Vol. 15, No. 29 (July 20, 1992).
9. J. Madeleine Nash, "When Love Is Exhausted," *Time* (April 6, 1992).

Chapter 1

1. Michael McCarthy, "Learning to Accept the Inevitable," *Los Angeles Times,* (August 27, 1991) E1.

Chapter 3

1. *Worst Pills, Best Pills: The Older Adult's Guide to Avoiding Drug-Induced Death or Illness,* Public Citizen Health Research Group, 1988.
2. Jane E. Brody, "The Elderly Find Medications Can Mingle Danger with Hope," *The New York Times* and *The Orange County Register* November 27, 1988), E12.
3. Brian S. Katcher, *Prescription Drugs: An Indispensable Guide for People over 50* (Athenaeum, 1988).
4. Brody.
5. Helene Lipton, M.D. and Philip Lee, M.D., "Drugs and the Elderly: Clinical, Social, and Policy Perspectives" (Stanford University Press, 1988) from "The Elderly Find Medications Can Mingle Danger with Hope," by Jane E. Brody,

The New York Times and *The Orange County Register* (November 27, 1988).
6. Ibid.
7. Margo McCaffrey, R.N., M.S.; Marion E. Morra, M.A.; Jody Gross, R.N., M.S.N.; and Derry Ann Moritz, R.N., M.S., "Dealing with Pain," American Cancer Society, Connecticut Division, Inc., Yale Comprehensive Cancer Center, 59.
8. *Questions and Answers about Pain Control,* The National Cancer Institute, Bethesda, Md. 20205.
9. McCaffrey, et. al.
10. *Questions and Answers about Pain Control.*
11. McCaffrey, et al.

Chapter 4
1. Alana Peters, Care Options.
2. "HICAP: Much Needed Program," *Seniors Chronicle* (San Clemente and San Juan Capistrano, Calif., March 1992), 6.
3. Marilyn Ditty, Ph.D. and Zondra Knapp, Ph.D., "Caregiving: Plan Early," *Seniors Chronicle* (San Clemente and San Juan Capistrano, Calif., January 1992), 1.
4. Ibid.
5. Ibid.
6. National Academy of Elder Law Attorneys, Inc., Tucson, Arizona (602) 881-4005.
7. Excerpted from "Your Health Care: Who Will Decide When You Can't?" California Medical Association, P.O. Box 7690, San Francisco, Calif. 94120-7690. (415) 882-5175.
8. Russell Chandler, "Religion Confronts Euthanasia," *Los Angeles Times* (November 2, 1991), A1.
9. Ibid.
10. Ibid.

Chapter 5
1. Some information adapted from *Nutrition Prescriptives,* Woodland Hills, California.

Chapter 6

1. Russell Chandler, "Nurses Become Health Ministers," *Los Angeles Times* (June 19, 1991), A1.
2. Ibid.
3. Marsha Fowler, R.N., M. Div., Ph.D., Director of the Parish Nursing Program, Azusa Pacific University, Azusa, California.
4. Ibid.
5. Ibid.

Chapter 7

1. *Modern Maturity*, California state election insert (October–November 1992).
2. James M. Gomez, "Home Medical Care Industry Showing Strong Vital Signs," *Los Angeles Times* (June 21, 1992), D1.
3. Ibid.
4. Ibid.
5. Ibid.
6. Jerry Holderman, "A Balance of Give and Take," *Los Angeles Times* (September 16, 1992), E1.
7. Ibid.
8. Lovola W. Burgess, "Long-Term Care: Now There's Help," *Modern Maturity* (October–November 1992), 6.
9. *Modern Maturity* (December–January 1993), 5.
10. Ibid.
11. Robert Lewis, "Iowa: Back to the Future," *AARP Bulletin* (November 1992), Vol. 33, No. 10), 1.
12. Ibid.
13. Ibid.
14. Ibid.
15. National Association of Private Geriatric Care Managers, 655 North Alvernon, Suite 108, Tucson, Ariz. 85711; (602) 881-8008.
16. Leslie Berkman and Davan Mahraj, "Growing Too Old or Too Ill for the Retirement Village," *Los Angeles Times* (May 4, 1992), A1.

17. Phyllis Brill, "When It's Time to Let Go," *Los Angeles Times* (January 26, 1992), E7.
18. Ruth M. Bathauer, *Parent Care* (Ventura, Calif.: Regal Books, 1992), 141. Used by permission.
19. Brill.
20. Phyllis Brill, adapted from "Tips May Ease the Pain of Making Decisions," *Los Angeles Times* (January 26, 1992), E7.
21. Sherry Angel, "For Elderly in Crisis, Ombudsmen Can Be Lifeline," *Los Angeles Times* (October 2, 1991), E1.
22. Ibid.
23. Illinois Council for Long-Term Care. (312) 478-6613.
24. Berkman and Maharaj.
25. Ibid.
26. "NBC Dateline," June 6, 1992.
27. Michael McCarthy, "Learning to Accept the Inevitable," *Los Angeles Times* (August 27, 1991), E1.
28. Ibid.
29. Ibid.
30. Ibid.
31. Declan Walsh, M.D., Director of the Cleveland Clinic.

Chapter 8
1. Philippians 1:21.
2. 1 Corinthians 15:26.
3. Quoted from a personal letter, names changed.
4. Sarah Jorunn Ricketts, condensed from *The Christian Herald* (September 1988). Used by permission.
5. Joseph Bayly, *The Last Thing We Talk About* (Elgin, Ill.: David C. Cook, 1977), 52. Used by permission.
6. John Claypool, *Tracks of a Fellow Struggler—How to Handle Grief* (Dallas: Word, Inc.). Used by permission.
7. Joseph Bayly, *Heaven* (Elgin, Ill.: David C. Cook, 1977). Used by permission.
8. Psalm 23:4-6.

Chapter 9
1. Lanie Jones, "Caregiver 'Burnout' Hits Many, Experts Say," *Los Angeles Times,* (April 27, 1992), B1.

2. Ibid.
3. Ibid.
4. Sherry Angel, "Care-Givers Often Neglect Somebody: Themselves," *Los Angeles Times* (May 22, 1991), E3.
5. Jones.
6. Ibid.
7. "Caregivers Caught in Trap," *Seniors Chronicle,* San Clemente, San Juan Capistrano, Calif. (October 1991), 1.
8. Jerry Holderman, "A Balance of Give and Take," *Los Angeles Times,* (September 16, 1992), E1.
9. Ibid.
10. "Aging, Living, and Caring: A Handbook for Elders, Families and Friends," (TRIMS Gerontology Center, Houston, Texas. Adapted from *The Orange County Register,* (November 15, 1992), M.
11. "Fitness," *Modern Maturity* (December 1992–January 1993), 29.
12. Marilyn Ditty, Ph.D. and Zondra Lewis Knapp, Ph.D., *The Daughter Trap* (Smith Gibbs, 1993).

Chapter 10
1. Barbara Deane, *Caring for Your Aging Parents: When Love Is Not Enough* (NavPress, 1989).

Chapter 11
1. "Spirituality Fosters Caring, Study Says," Associated Press, *Los Angeles Times* (October 3, 1992), B8.
2. Ibid.
3. Ibid.
4. Ibid.
5. Ibid.
6. Nehemiah 8:10.
7. Robertson McQuilkin, "Ministry or Family: The Choice," *Leadership Journal,* Wheaton, Ill. (Spring Quarter 1991), 39. Used by permission.
8. Nathan W. Goff, "A Lifetime Lesson Learned from Pain," *Stillpoint,* Gordon College, Wenham, Mass. (Spring 1991), 27. Used by permission.

230 Caring for Those Who Can't

9. G. Lloyd Carr and Gwendolyn C. Carr, *The Fierce Good-bye: Hope in the Wake of Suicide* (Downers Grove, Ill.: Intervarsity Press, 1990). Used by permission.

10. Karen Lundell Faul, "Continuing to Live . . . One Day at a Time," *Stillpoint*, Gordon College, Wenham, Mass. (Spring, 1991), 13. Used by permission.

12. Charles H. Spurgeon, *Morning and Evening* (Peabody, Mass.: Hendrickson Publishers), 29.

14. Jack R. Taylor, *The Hallelujah Factor* (Nashville, Tenn.: Broadman Press, 1983). Used by permission.

15. 2 Chronicles 20:9, 12.

17. 2 Chronicles 20:15.

18. 2 Chronicles 20:21.

19. 2 Chronicles 20:21, kjv.